Life is when love is having a dream

For more inspiration, art, and new book
releases, follow the author on Instagram:
kimgromoll

Kim Nina Gromoll

WHEN THE RAIN BOWS TO YOUR TEARS

An Awakening Journey
through the Self, Gaia, and the Ocean of Emotion

Imprint

Production & Publisher:
BoD · Books on Demand GmbH,
In de Tarpen 42,
22848 Norderstedt,
bod@bod.de

Print:
Libri Plureos GmbH,
Friedensallee 273,
22763 Hamburg

Copyright © 2025 by Kim Nina Gromoll

Author:
Kim Nina Gromoll

Cover & Illustration:
Kim Nina Gromoll

Title:
When the Rain Bows to Your Tears -
An Awakening Journey through the Self, Gaia, and the Ocean of Emotion

ISBN: 978-3-7693-2159-3

www.kimgromoll.com
www.kimgromollpoetry.com

For your dreaming heart

Table of Contents

Table of Contents

Part III: The Void

Chapter 7: The Eye of the Storm

Chapter 8: Silent Lake

Chapter 9: Unconditional Love

Part IV: Second Birth

Chapter 10: Emerging From the Womb once again, but this Time it's my Own

Table of Contents

The Round Table

Growth and integration happen in the spiraling flow of nature. It's the reviewing of one's themes on repeat, each time with an expanded awareness. Infinity as the continuity of ebb & flood, while we rise in our sense of being. Every end is a beginning, and every beginning is an end, but in the end there is no such thing.

While we are the silent observer in the center, we expand in ripples and circles, experiencing life and learning more about ourselves. Time is like that. Like the path of the spiral that gives us the opportunity to undergo personal change and transformation, while in reality it all happens simultaneously, in the eternal moment of your being, the now. Your soul is the director of that placed awareness– your persona, which you perceive yourself as. The pointer of the clock, until you can see wholly.

The chapters and texts in this book hold feelings and experiences that I find myself revisiting. I keep re-arriving at self-judgement, joy, pain, and self-love. Even though the book is built in a linear way, I experience it like a spinning force. All states are valid as I go back and forth between them. All those themes sit together at a round table as the tablet that I am. Like an ancient disk, telling the story of my own creation through my inscriptions.

Acknowledgments

Thank you to each—

My family for everything. My mother, the guiding light, for always believing in me. My father, the guiding darkness, for loving me through his sorrow. My friend, the Weeping Willow, for standing still with me. Aphrodite for calling me home. Eka for seeing my heart before I could see it. Kimonos Art Center & Rally Space for being my first stepping stone into the new. Melle & Don Diego—my dear tigers, for loving me unconditionally. Kelly for being the first person to have read this book. Grace for taking my picture. Qua, all my guides, angels, and teachers, for navigating me through life and this endless awakening. Mother Earth, water, breath, all plants and animals, for grounding and connecting me with truth. All my friends for accepting me and my insanity and for bringing me so much laughter. My workplace for offering me so many ways to reflect upon myself. My self-chosen hometown, Maastricht, for giving me my first sense of freedom. Poetry and art for the ability to express myself. And me, for trusting, loving, and being; for hoping, feeling, and seeing; for growing, dreaming, and leaning in.

Introduction

This book shares personal realizations about existence on deeper levels. Paths that brought me into the very fundament of my being and soul through the emotions that seem to control all life. But this book is not about control; it's about surrender. A journey that started with being born and continues with being born, while revealing new ways to navigate oneself through the ocean of emotion. To face all reflections through the connections with others. It brought me to the very core of everything and nothing—the void. There I had to create my own meaning and purpose after having acknowledged the overwhelming insanity of a higher consciousness talking to me through me. A larger part of myself and everyone else.

These texts are not for the fainthearted. This book is confronting; it's a love story, and I hope that it makes you fall in love with yourself and the world just as it did for me. But it requires you to drop all conditioned beliefs in order to perceive the answers to those questions that you have carried with you since forever.

Please note that I don't intend for you to find yourself in all the statements and claims that I make in this book. This is my perception of reality and truth for the moments in which I wrote them. It may change over time, and it might not be true for you. I am sharing my story here, and if you can relate to parts of it, it might help you to understand yourself better.

Part I

First Birth

The Ocean of Emotion

Dark and Light as in: The Search for Self and Love in the Mirror of the World.

What is my Longing?

What is my longing?
Is it my hope and my dream?
Is it an urge to escape the now?
An urge to hide or to grow?
An urge to nurture, coming from my soul?

Aphrodite and the Child

Aphrodite emerged from the sea and took the ocean with her,
in her body of creation and in her breath.

Now the ocean is everywhere and always was.

She gave birth to herself
over and over again,
through earth and heaven,
mother and father,
body and mind.

She is the love that explores through every emotion.

She steps out of the ocean to breathe and drowns in it again.
In the fluctuating states of the elements that perform an endless dance
through the constructs of reality,
through the forms of creation.

She is in us, and we are in her.

Born from the marriage of salt and water,
the union of two that attract and dissolve one another,
while together birthing as the womb of infinite possibilities.

As the liquid field of mind and dreams,
wherein the child wants to experience it all.
It is playing so deeply that it forgets
that it is dreaming and falls asleep,
now ruled by unconscious currents.

Nostalgia

Sometimes it's weird, you know, being an adult and all. On the days off, you are at home alone. Nobody tells you when to wake up, when to clean up, when, and what to eat up. You enjoy the freedom, and at the same time you long for the care that you had back then, when you wanted to control everything, while now you want to lose it again. You miss the bedtime stories, the tucking in, the warm bath, and the kitchen cabinet candy robbing. You miss the lonely weekend mornings until midday, while you silently watched television or climbed the backyard tree on your secret mission. You miss the weekends at Grandma's and Grandpa's, where you spend all day with the dogs. Your best pet friends—the only heartful friends, because nobody else understands. You tasted grandpa's apple juice knowing it was beer, and you enjoyed kitchen sessions of fly smashing. Each one meant at least a 2-cent cashing.

All the good that you remember, while you still longed to grow up. I guess I forgot to mention the screaming, the cries, and the pain-laden expressions of my parents past. But it didn't last. It got better, just not so fast. Or at least it changed from one sea of hurt into the next. And it was me swimming in it with them. Nobody to blame. I just felt so much shame that I thought it was mine. School wasn't great, and then their split-up happened that felt like somebody had ripped out my heart. No longer able to show all my love. This was the first time that I felt totally encapsulated by the unknown, so very different from the dark time in my mother's womb. I hear it and hear it and hear it. It's not your fault; we love you always. Things will be better; don't put your breath on hold. And the new guy, the new kids, how can all that fit into my mother's heart? Where am I? First it was just me; now it has to fit four more. What's that supposed to mean? Now I know that love can only multiply, but back then it all felt like a lie. Betrayed my little heart, and my innocence turned towards the dark.

It may not seem quite Real

Bleeding wounds,
covered with anger, lethargy, addiction, and fear.

How can my father be when he drowns in his own grief,
deep inside for the rest of his life?
What would he even be if it weren't for me?
Was I a spark of hope, to feel love?

But that's over now.
Drowned again, not only in losing others but losing himself in the ocean of pain.
The body slowly suffocating,
without breath.
It got too dark for him.

Eyes filled with clouds where his inner child lurks behind,
Peter Pan of some kind.

I cannot stand to see you suffer like this.
Like the parent that wants only happiness for his child.
The father that I knew, the one in the pictures,
smiling, young, handsome, and creative.
This memory seems only alive in your voice on the phone,
bringing me back to a time when I used to feel alone.

I want to keep you safe, but I can't.
You have to own up to yourself,
because pain is not all that is,
and life is much bigger than just this.

I accept you now for the emotions that you chose,
to drown and sink again to the bottom of the ocean
into the tears of your soul,
where it's so dark that you forgot that you are whole.

And maybe it's me that is projecting all those emotions onto you,
creating a story in my head that isn't true.

Because you won't speak to me about how you feel,
and I don't dare to ask, still hoping you might heal.

But I see and I am grateful for what you did for me,
showing me how I don't want to be.

I love you nonetheless,
through all that disconnects.

I came through you, and I can see it now too.
And even if I cannot make you be someone else,
I will try to heal your wounds through myself.

I will not lie; if you die,
I don't know how I will feel.
It may not seem quite real.

Somehow it already feels as if you are dead.
The father that I knew, that I once had.

Still, this death cannot keep us apart,
from being us
—freeing—
being our beating hearts.

A space to balance back into the ocean.
A space that holds every possible notion.
Everywhere and in us always,
just lighter.

Death as a space for our breath.

It's not somewhere other than here,
but it's a part of all that holds no more fear.

Completely 'In Love'

How do you define love? Is it about what you desire to receive in actions from another? Actions, thoughts, and feelings are inherently linked to each other. They are the three corners of the triangle that make you whole. But what meaning do you give the feeling that you consider to be love? And is that concept of yours really love, or is it built from what you've learned to believe about it? Can it be more? Can it be different?

How do you want to feel when you consider yourself to be in love? Is it the fairytale version? Or can you also accept and surrender to everything else that comes with it? In every emotion that continuously transforms your being. You have to admit that you enjoy feelings of sadness, anger, and grief, even if you might label them as bad. They liberate you, they are necessary, and they allow you to process the intensity of holding onto all that is subject to change.

Are you willing to surrender to the transformational and unavoidable power of your love? With every moment, every place, and every person, through all the feelings that occur within?

Blind Birth

Before you were born,
your light was so bright and intense,
that it was blinding your sense
of what it means to be.

Born as a human you've received the gift of a blind mind
in order to be able to see the dark
and feel the heavy beats of your heart.

And the growing dark beliefs of mind
are now trying to betray your heart.
The shadow that wants to conquer its counterpart.

But the shadow can never defeat the light,
as its essence lies in the opposing site.

Mama

Thank you for your selflessness,
so that I could have a connection with my father.
Thank you for teaching me compassion
with your heart that feels so strong and upset
about all the dark decisions in this global web.

Thank you for showing me how you stood up for yourself,
how you gave to yourself,
and how you stepped away.

You did not know any better before that,
but everything happens for a reason,
so there is no room for regret.

Thank you for giving me my brother
and for showing how abundant your love is as a mother.

Thank you for being the father that I no longer have,
the father that others seem to have,
while mine drowns in its wounds.

Thank you for making me cry
when you say what you always said,
that I have to hold my head up high,

and that you love me.

But it's tough for me.
I don't want to hear it.
I don't know how to say it back,
and I feel the persistence of this uncomfortable regret.

You speak to the child in me,
and she can hear you so clearly.
But I don't want to remember.
I don't want to cry again as I did for so many years.

Dried up now,
all those tears.
Frozen,
all those fears.

I prefer to tell you in whispering words,
for they make my voice feel so loud.

Can you hear me now?
Are you proud?

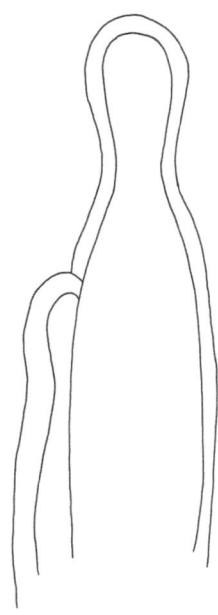

Cut the Bullshit

I just want to
cut the bullshit that I am telling myself.
cut the bullshit that I am making myself feel.
cut the bullshit that makes me wanna hide.
cut the bullshit that feels so wrongfully right.

I just want to
cut the bullshit that keeps me entrapped.
cut the bullshit that I long to forget.
cut the bullshit that makes me reject me.
cut the bullshit that is my self-inflicted pain.

I just want to
cut the bullshit that operates below my natural domain.
cut the bullshit that feels so truthfully wrong.
cut the bullshit that takes room in my heart.
cut the bullshit in which I no longer want to play a part.

I just want to
cut the bullshit that I've owned for so long.
cut the bullshit that feels like it won't ever be gone.
cut the bullshit that belongs in the past.
cut the bullshit that is not supposed to last.

What do you dream Of?

What does love mean to you?

What does life mean to you?

What does the ocean mean to you?
What do mountains mean to you?

What does the horizon mean to you?
What does dusk mean to you?

What do others mean to you?

What does the sun mean to you?
What does the night mean to you?

What do you dream of?

What does your past mean to you?
What does this moment mean to you?

What do you dream of?

What does planet Earth mean to you?
What does your body mean to you?

What does art mean to you?
What do children mean to you?

What do your thoughts mean to you?
What does your breath mean to you?

What does death mean to you?

What do you dream of?

How to Swim

The Mask

Your heart, guarded by fear,
freezing each tear into a mask.

The longer you wear it, the more you forget to take it off.
No longer soft but sore is your core,
and it will hurt even more the longer you wait
to uncover your fate.

Are you afraid your current escape will disappear,
holding the risk that might leave you with nothing else but fear?

How does your mask sustain?
Is there a special flame that you can hold it into, or some type of superglue?
Do you give it a good night's rest, or did it pass some special tests?
How many years of guarantee?
When will it break?

Aren't you afraid of what you might see when it puts you down on one knee?
To surrender.
Are you willing to rise with the splendor
of your soul?

Do you really want to know yourself?
Then you have to show yourself.
Because you owe it to your soul to finally embrace your whole.

Are you ready to be teared down into the depths of the melting water?
The pieces of your mask,
frozen tears that dissolve into lakes, rivers, and rain,
releasing the ocean of your pain.
So deep, dark, and blue, it's you.

Face all that you are,
every soft part, every wound, and every scar.

Stop the play of hide and seek.
Can't you see how deep you bleed?

Can you swim and bathe in the blood?
In every wound, in your own love, and all of your flaws?
It's not easy and might not feel light,
but after a while it brings peace to your internal fight.

And when the sunlight touches your water,
you will see the wholeness of that fear in its parts.
Like a crowd of harmless tiny fish,
protecting themselves, their lives, and their hearts,
together looking like big aggressive sharks.

Now a new horizon appears,
right above the ocean of your fears.
It opens the door to the endlessness of your core.

Can you forgive and give yourself permission?
It doesn't mean that you no longer bleed,
but you will now know that you are complete,
with every wound and every scar, as the beautiful person that you are.

My Biggest Insecurity

I call her my biggest insecurity. She who lived in my belly for so many years. Afraid to be seen. She did not feel as a part of me, but as an unwanted extension that lived attached and free. Still, it was her with whom I've identified the most. I did my utmost best to not love her—myself, me as the embodiment of insecurity and shame. Who is to blame? Is it my family and the days of judgment that I used to face? They did it to feel less worse about themselves, and I felt worse again, because through my birth I relate to them. This is not how I wanted to be seen, but it was the only way in which I saw myself. Others were not judging me; only I was, for whom I've been. And sometimes I still am. It's the one big shadow that I carry with me each day since I can't even remember when. Where did it come from? I only know now that my body was protecting me, holding on to this dense energy that physically intensified the shame and guilt, thinking that's just the way I've been built. When I looked at old pictures, how perfect I was, so thin, but the lifestyle back then towards my body and soul was a sin. I did not care how I looked, and now I do not know how to not care while always in despair.

Through her, the discomfort and search for a cure led and connected me to pursue the most pure. Pure and real as the way that I wanted to feel. It was the nurture and medicine of nature—Mother Earth, who satisfied my inner thirst. I felt so much better energetically, but I did not feel much better about how I looked in my nurturing center. Why did I always want what I didn't seem to have? Why couldn't I feel how much I was truly blessed? Beyond the end, this is all just a little test for me to grow from the past havocs of my soul. And the blessing that I tried to resist is the gift to be me the way that I exist.

I could not accept my form because I wanted to fit into the beauty norm. Thorns that I turned against myself. And even when something seemed to work, there was no balance. But my cells were begging me to have faith. Torn apart between my body's voice and my self-hating heart. To have faith in the sacred garden and in the infinity of time, knowing that in the endless end I will always just be fine.

Nurtured through Gaia so pure, there couldn't be any other cure. And it was not only in her but in myself, the green heart as the key to everlasting health. To love me unconditionally as the only possible way to be free.

The Waves follow each Other

The waves follow each other.
From outside in
I receive them through my skin.
And from the inside out I am the ocean and pulse myself,
overflowing other islands and touching their wells.

From helping a friend relieve unease
I encountered a woman lying on the streets.
Deep sadness arrived at my shore.
Is it coming from outside or from my own core?

Did the one person's unease transform
or was it just passed on?
Can feelings not change and instead only travel further in motion,
and why did I feel of both a portion?

Seconds later a swarm of swallows floats through the sky,
moving in unity like waves,
so perfect without mistakes.
Their freedom becomes mine.
Their joy feels so sublime.

I am in between.
I feel each scene happening above and down here.
I feel the beauty of both carried in a single tear.

I follow the street
where the large building is touching the sky.
It's so ugly, I wonder why.
What does ugly even mean,
and am I judging this scene?

But before I can think of an answer,
I see the sunset waking up in its windows.

Helping Hands

Why is it that we wish to accomplish things on our own?
Why is it that we don't want to ask for help?

There is a reason for being in this world together.
Not to fight each other, not to win or lose,
but to grow as a community within the one planet.

There is a reason for your desire to offer help when you see someone
struggling. It's not only for them to feel a sense of gratitude,
because you can feel it too. That's when you meet each other in the heart,
in opportunity, in growth, and the uplift of life.

As much as you cannot save the whole world on your own,
you cannot save yourself from yourself on your own.

This world is made for connection out of love.

Because of Love

If you fear or act through any emotion, you still act that way because of love. Each emotion is directly linked to it. But you resist it. You resist acknowledging your own center and essence. Why? Because you associate your wound and the layers of emotions that protect it as your home. Its familiarity. Shed the layers, embrace your wound, and let it breathe. Let it reveal its essence to you. Feel it and find yourself in it. The beauty and love that you are. The child that hides within. Let it out and show it that it is safe now. The child that is your heart. The child that you once were. Become the child again, and you become the love that you are longing for.

Body

Am I the space inside my body?
The connection, attraction, and affection?
The love between my cells?
But also the separation between those that are not supposed to meet,
to keep the system alive and let it thrive?

Every bite that you take should nurture you.
Not only your emotions and soul,
but your layers of body as a whole.

Not to fill the holes, but to sustain,
so you can keep playing this game.

Towards what side do you lean?
Too much or too little seems so extreme.
It's the ever-going search for balance,
in which you have to accept where you are at.

Don't reject the other side nor your inside,
because it's in all the parts where your truth hides.

You are the mother and father in each degree.
Your body – the wise child, connected to the wild.
Consuming and believing everything that you do, say, and think,
but listen to its earthly wisdom in order to be completely in sync.

There is an endless love inside each cell that only wants you to be well.
Because you are their well, and you are their heaven.
You are their sky in which each part is longing to fly.

And who doesn't love to watch the sun rise and fall?
It's the essence of your all.
Make sure that you let the sun rise for each cell.
Don't make their life a living hell.

Wounds

When you are born, you are the center between your parents and a representation of the love that created you. Because that's the essence of the creator and the creation. You are born from the cosmic womb and, while being a baby and small child, are perceived as this innocent miracle. A beautiful wonder that reminds each one of their origin.

In the process of growing up, you expand and experience the whole range of emotions that existence in this realm is all about. It's the parts that shape your fluid totality. You learn to navigate, process, and handle those emotions by the examples that were given to you. When your parents are not in balance with themselves, you might experience more imbalance and conflicts within. Caused through their and your ancestors emotional inheritance. Distortions that you inherited through the body and through your DNA. In those, cells serve as time capsules for all the wounds that are waiting to be acknowledged.

During your life you keep returning to your inner wounds to take on their wisdom as they nurture you in the darkness until you have transformed and alchemized the past. Heal and feel them not only for yourself, but for your children and others. Because when you heal your own wounds, you are healing theirs.

Solitude

Oh my dear solitude,
when I am in a crowd, I long for it to be just you and me.

You are the empty.
Within you I am free,
because you created me,
and through you I can shape who I want to be,
the empty fullness of me.

Oh my dear solitude,
within you I love to play wild music,
and dance through your halls,
along those walls that I call home.

But when we are alone, there are also moments
in which I avoid seeing and hearing.
When no solace is nearing,
it feels so intense to just be,
full of emptiness, like a vacuum.
No longer able to breathe in or out,
in this motionless cloud of silence, so loud.

To sit and observe all the nothing, as part of me.
All the emotions that seem so dense,
like a chaos that I wish to cleanse.

Like the snake that swims in her impersonal lake,
blinded by the dark seafloor and the bright sky.
She is the surface tension in between low and high.

A membrane so dense,
that she has to perform a dance,
to shed herself again and again,
to release the skin from head to tail,
to feel and to grow,
to break out of her own jail,
and to learn how to flow.

My heart is urging me to no longer fight my darkness and my light
but to create the outside through the emptiness within,
to widen my horizon by shedding my old skin.

Oh my dear solitude,
I no longer want to be alone.
I love you, but can we please invite someone
to sit with us on our spacious throne?
Someone from outside, who feels at home in my emptiness, just as in their own.

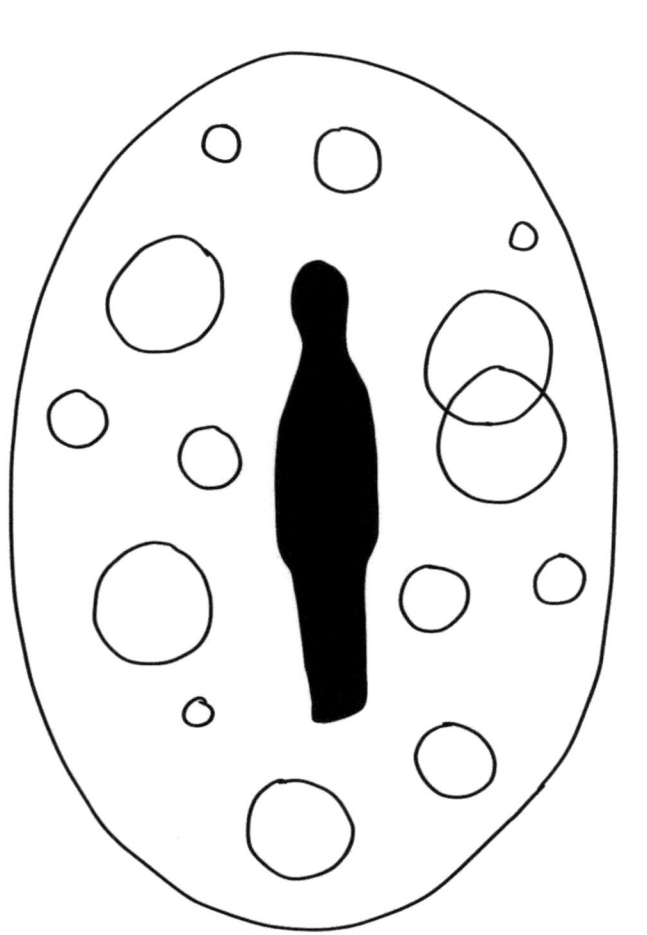

How to Dive

Pearls

I had a dream one night that showed me that pearls are the true glass of the ocean. Pearls are produced by seashells, scarlike, to protect the shell from the outside while harvested by humans for their natural beauty. The normal shell consists of the same material as the pearl, but it's not valued the same.

There is beauty in your pain, in your tears, and in your scars. In all parts of your being. And the emotional wounds reveal your true core once you let them bleed, breathe, and heal naturally. Honest and real in their essence and inherently connected to the salty and deep, dark ocean out of which you came. The cosmic womb that has many appearances and layers in its different states of being.

So why do you hide your beauty, and why do you try to cover up those tears? Nobody will steal them, because they are your most authentic self and your essence. And nobody can steal your essence, nor diminish your existence. But your ocean needs to flow in order to be alive.

Everyone that makes you cry doesn't know that they actually give you the gift of being your true self. To release, breathe, and purify the parts inside that the other person has reflected to you. They give you the gift to connect to your origin and beauty. Whether through the positive or the negative.

You have to put the pieces back together that are inherently linked to the love that you are. Being your own womb. And every connection gives to you what your soul needs in order to root back into the wholeness of your being. It's there to remind you of who you are, where you have been, and where you want to be in the journey of finding yourself through your pearls.

You are the Tree

Don't try to untangle your roots and emotions in order to create a clearer structure of what or who you are. Clarity comes when you loosen your focus and
breathe in the mist of connection. Through your roots, you absorb the liquid,
solid, and loving foundations of Mother Earth. She helps you to become just like
the tree, and so does your past. Try to feel the wholeness of your roots and what
they do for you. To grow stronger by grounding you in your origin. Your stem is
the heart in between the light and the dark. In between body and mind. The Now
is the I that holds the potential of your personal sky. We are always rooted in the
dark soil that feeds us, and we are always dancing between summer and winter.
Inside and out. Embrace and acknowledge your personal history and past to see
where you want to grow from here. Towards what future, towards what part of
the sky? The horizon is endless, and the sun returns every day to remind you of
what's possible while nurturing you through your leaves. Until you are ready to
be vulnerable and reveal your innermost essence—flowers.

And if you've grown thorns, can you embrace them too? They are your softness
that carefully tries to reach out into the world, longing for connection through
its own protection.

As the tree enables our reality, can you let yourself be nurtured by the dark and
the light? Can you transform your soil into a breath of fresh air? Can you al-
chemize the cycles of feelings, thoughts, and beliefs by photosynthesizing them
through your leaves?

Once you learn how to grow and respond to your inner landscape in a harmoni-
ous way, you will attract birds to sit in your crown. You become a home through
every season. A stage for the most sacred sounds.

I Died

Layers of emotions, behaviors, age, looks, and actions.
Layers of lies.
All infused with truth.
But where does truth come from?
There is nothing that is not true,
because everything that exists,
does so for you.

I push it all to the outside, like prayers.
Onto others. All the thickening layers.
What do I try to slay, and who do I actually betray?
Projecting. Protecting. Staying safe.
But I also want to free myself.

Others immediately throw them back at me.
Those truths that I don't want to see.
The only thing that I want to know is where I actually begin.
Is it somewhere underneath the layers of my skin?

To go there I have to dissolve each layer that holds a terrible truth.
I refuse. But it's looping back at me, until I am willing to see.
Willing to feel.
Willing to be.
Willing to kneel.
Willing to love it for what it did for me
on this path of rediscovery.

From dark to light organically,
just like the tree.
And I stay grounded now,
knowing how I can grow.
Not avoiding my roots,
because they're bringing me fruits.

Dying many times again through each skin.
Death as the door that leads me back to whom I've always been.

And the doors do not disappear,
I can now look through many of them from right here.
To connect with others from within
instead of through each true fake skin.

I reached myself and continue to do.
What about you?
Do you want to feel and be?
Are you longing to dive in and see?
Into your own womb and ocean with deepest devotion?

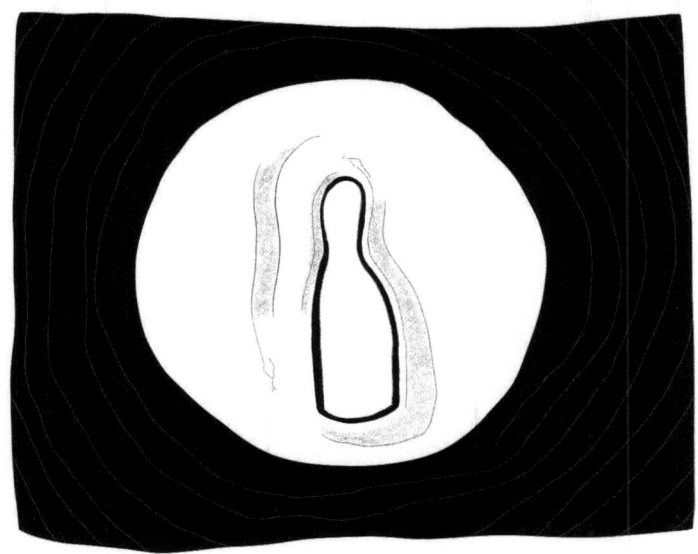

Can You lose Yourself in Love?

Can you lose yourself in love?
You are already lost in it. We are always searching for love. Everything that we do is related to this desire. As if we don't know that we are swimming in its creation. In all the emotions that originate in love. Lost in a knot, trying to untangle, not realizing that we are that thread. And that thread is love itself, which created all the crossroads. A thread that has no end nor beginning. Always flowing back and forth through the void and universal heart where each emotion connects.

You are lost in yourself because love is not something outside of you. You've created all of this. Longing for yourself. Thinking that you find it somewhere else. Life is the path of death. Shedding versions and walls of personalities that keep you from expanding your heart. Until you die completely. Until you find and love yourself again, as the space of your heart. You are the pulse, the core, and creation itself. Expanding. Growing. Birthing.

Shadowed Dream

Your biggest insecurity is the shadow of your biggest dream. That, what you desire most. You might not even be fully aware of it because your mind is telling lies about your dream and inner child. It holds the shadow of your heart, turning the dream into an unattainable idea and the dreamer into a fool.

How long do you want to keep living in the shadows? You are the sun, the flame, and the fire that created all the ashes and shades of grey. Old versions needed to be burnt in order to nurture you as your own soil. And now your moist shadows are being exposed to your fire. Drying, burning, and supporting your growth while integrating as transformed particles into your new structure. The transformation of your inner world. Like sharp pieces of glass being heated through your unseen sun and melting back together into the one perfect pearl that holds your prophecy.

Uncentered Balance

Separation and duality can only be experienced when we perceive something else as different from us. When we try to acquire a certain emotional state from an often conditioned way of feeling. We long for joy, love, and happiness in this very moment while placing ourselves in separation from it, believing that it doesn't belong to us. And that very belief of feeling unworthy is the actual state that we try to reject, which makes it a static constant. A self-summoned state through which we express ourselves into reality and actions. We express the avoidance and the judgment that occur within while in reality we only avoid and judge ourselves, as we identify with that very emotion.

When you consciously feel the current emotion, it feels seen, softens, and dissolves back into the void. Into your personal aether. A process of transmuting and alchemizing the here and now through allowance. And from your void, feelings of relief, peace, and gratitude can appear in you as the very joy that you were looking for. It just required each emotion to be admired.

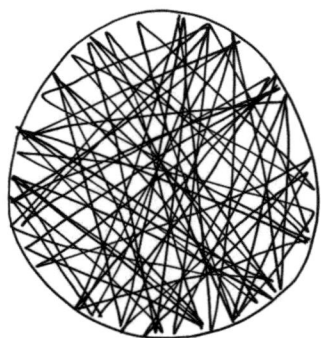

Gratitude

Feel gratitude for every situation and experience. Feel it for the positive and the negative. Not for the sake of the circumstances or how it should feel according to your mind. But for the sake of knowing that the outside projection of your inner world brings you whatever you require in order to find balance and healing. If that's another trigger, then so be it. Let it show you what you haven't been working on. Let the moonlight illuminate your haunting shadows and let the purging begin. Through gratitude you allow yourself to receive what you need the most. Through gratitude you allow the chaos to sort itself anew. You allow the unpleasant to do its work until your space of being is purified so much that you can see and feel the love from which you grew.

Elemental Motion

I carry all parts,
all versions,
all shapes, and each form.
All that has ever been born.

solid — plasma — liquid — gas

I am the ocean that's dancing through each state,
through every element that I create.
And the speed of the dance and how it transforms
is ruled by nature's magical norms.

Every degree reveals a part of the mystery of how I came to be.

I cannot seem to fully understand,
always returning back to myself in the end.
If it's cold, I yearn for connection,
to touch and hug; please warm me up.
When it's too warm, I desire the wind and sea
to cool down my body's degree.

And my heart…
As a young child, I used to be a spark.
A potential fire wanting to grow higher.
Then for many years I felt so cold and lonely without hope.
But that cold wind let my fire breathe,
eventually taking me away from the unease.

Able to see where my flames were longing to be,
longing to go,
to grow once again
from low
to high
to low
to high
to low,
awaiting the next airflow.

And I realized that I am not only the fire but also the breath,
able to take me out of my own depth.

I am not only the bird
but also the feather that is floating free and high through the sky,
until I return to the ground
where my body flows back into the ocean of elemental motion.

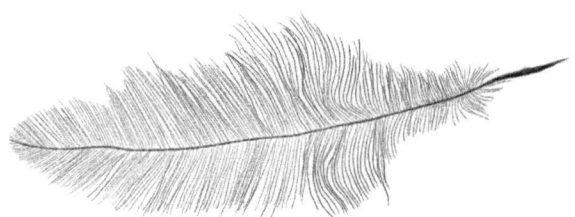

Your Inner Calling

There comes a moment in life when your dream and inner calling start to knock on the door. You might have always felt what your particular purpose is, but if you did not believe in yourself or you were unaware of it altogether, then it will show up as an overwhelming surprise. It feels so exciting and scary when your dream starts to materialize itself into your reality. Unknowingly you did everything necessary to reach this new level, but now you ask yourself if you are truly ready. Ready for the success. Ready for the money. Ready for the love and ready for the responsibility that comes with your burning flame. Ready for the freedom that becomes yours only when you open up. To share your passion with the world, for the world. Your highest potential is to return to your soul's essence. To what brings you the most joy. Like the dense seed that longs to grow and the flower that wants to be expressed.

Part II

Dying

Drowning in the Fear

Take the most fearful Path, and it will lead You to Yourself.

Don't You feel Worthy?

You can't run away from your higher self, your soul's purpose, and your heart's desire. You probably try, but it will only make you cry even more. And it's okay if that's what you want to choose. It's a path that has an equal right to be. But would it be because you are afraid to lose yourself in the unknown? To fall back down from that part of yours that is your light, yet unseen? You can't lose the person that you are now, but you can make it your past, which is something that will forever last. As a memory and a dream that you have already seen. Now go and trust your wildest dreams ahead and believe in your heart.

Do you feel worthy of your own love?
I didn't. And I don't know why. I guess I just wasn't born that high. I didn't feel worthy, and I didn't feel hope. I felt disliked, lonely, stupid, and wrong. My best friend was hurting me to pretend and to rule. And I was not good enough for my father, but maybe I misunderstood, and all he wanted for me was to be good. To be at my best, guided to endure his endless test. Am I doing him wrong, and he just didn't know where his sense was coming from? Probably, but now I no longer hide, and he no longer speaks.

I know that my father loves me, and my friend was only scared, so she acted as if she didn't care. Both couldn't love themselves. I forgive you, and I forgive myself for trusting in what you let me believe, of being unworthy to receive. I observe, reflect, and reject what I don't want and need. I was the seed in the dark, but I am no longer tight, because now I absorb the sweetness from above. The sweet parts of love.

Trust your wishes and dreams, because when you run, it won't get any more fun. It may seem safe, but you will stay in the same place, and after a while, the comfort turns into a prison. Motionless and dead. Why won't you go ahead? Life is only about change. To experience and try. You cannot fail; you can only fly! It stays scary, because you don't know who and what you will carry. It's a journey that is lonely. At least that's how it seems when you look from here into the nothing—into the dark and the light. Both so dense and bright. You cannot see who, what, and where you will be. Only guided by your dream and the search for your own self-esteem. But with every step ahead, with every day and every night that you look back, it's no longer bright and deep.

The bridge that you are on has revealed the colors of your song. A rainbow, where the rain bows to your tears. And now there is no way that leads you back into the old, as long as you trust your heart of gold. It knows the way because its love is the start and the finish. Never able to diminish. If you follow it through high and low, your life will be in perfect flow. And the lows become the ebb. No longer so deep. Just a little dry when another sun is high. A break from the hike to replenish and reflect on the path that you are at.

What if...

Trust in the future as in the merging of hopes and beliefs. It's the balancing of the "What ifs". Trust feels impossible, but you are a master of it already. You trust so strongly in what you know and in what you have experienced before. Things labeled as negative through the definitions that you created. The fear that your future will be the same as your past hardships.

But what if you have the courage to trust your hopes and dreams? The ones that seem and stay unreal if you choose to continue the same way as yesterday. Can you feel safe being blind with open eyes before the new day begins? Or do you rather close your eyes in the darkness and continue the nightmare that is encouraging you to wake up? It's scary to look ahead and find a new path that you don't know yet. But isn't it even scarier to stay in the same place for the rest of your life? To end new days before they have even begun? Are you afraid to get your heart broken again? Those cracks are there on purpose. It's the shedding of your skin that is ready to break open completely. To reveal the newborn membrane of your heart and to expand its inner depth.

All experiences and emotions in this life are a blessing to find your truth. Fear will never leave, because it helps you, it loves you, and it has a right to be. But you have to discern when it's time to move up that new mountain. To have a view and show your fear the new horizon. You see from up there where you can and want to be. That road in the far is the path that begins in your heart. And your heart is the compass that leads you to inevitable bliss if you follow its guidance.

Boxes

Our essence and heart are only fragile when we try to control and protect them. When we build a box around it that doesn't allow for natural movement. Your heart becomes stiff and cannot follow its original motion and pulse. Let it guide you to where it longs to go. And you already know where it wants to take you, because you can feel the pull and attraction deep inside. Can you let go of that box of fear that is anchored in your past? Everything that has happened did so in order for you to question yourself and your true desires. It happened to strengthen your trust in the future through events of uncertainty. Events that were created to breathe out the sadness and to discard old layers, in order for your soul to get ready to shine the light of your heart into the world. A light unable to break and unable to diminish, but here for you to heal, love, and live in inner freedom. Because only then can you truly help others in the best possible way. Only then is everything possible.

Can you allow your heart to experience every part of its kingdom? Can you allow in what you feel drawn to and what certainly feels drawn to you? Or do you want to keep building boxes of fear and disconnection around your attraction? Let it all move through you; let it enter your wounds and feel the healing pain of that love. When you unbox yourself, the natural flow is what will make you feel effortlessly alive.

Golden Soul

What do you believe about yourself to be true that doesn't align with your heart? What beliefs in your mental construct create that fear and anxiety? What are you really afraid of? The push and pull happens between your mind and your heart. Between your negative ego and your higher self. Fear as your guide is showing you what you deeply long to transform in order to feel the freedom of your soul.

Become lucid and build your heaven on earth through the realization of your own worth. Nothing is too good to be true. Witness how everything that you need to know will flow through you in perfect timing with the infinite moment. If you follow the dream in your heart, you will find your tribe, unite, co-create, and ignite. To burn the old and build a new world from gold.

Heartbeat

Your inner child is living in your wound, afraid and hiding. But fear can't conquer curiosity, and so your innocent self sticks its head out from time to time. To breathe and to have a look at the scary and exciting freedom outside of that compressed comfort zone. Your wound needs to breathe too, but as long as your child is living in it, the wound keeps stretching. Insecurity is the illusion that only allows one to feel secure through seclusion, while in reality you are hiding from yourself. You are avoiding the confrontations that intensify if you don't change the beliefs that keep you stuck. And the outside world is showing you the perpetuating wealth of lack that you praise through your own negativity.

Expose yourself and look into your burning. You can't keep holding on to a single inner sound without allowing the other to come around. The other heartbeat that always has to follow. You need to breathe in and out while letting go of the doubt. Allow your being to spread its pulse. Find your rhythm and start to see the results. You will find others that resound, and together you create new melodies. But you have to allow yourself those first few beats of your heart. It's your soul's call that will be heard by the right people. They are the mirror and medicine for your wound. Helping you to step out of it and offering a view of yourself and the world through a different set of eyes. You are their medicine too. It's an exchange of hearts.

Nightmares

Do you choose to run away from yourself within your own infinity? Or do you allow in what you had thought of as punishments for past sin? Can you allow the cloud to cry and the wetness of the soil to evaporate into the sky?

You are no longer haunted in your dreams when you allow all the themes to tell their story. When you allow the demons to purify through your body.

They are the reflections of your pain, fear, and sorrow. Wanting to be seen and felt. Longed to be held like you long to be held.

But when you hide away, you will never be able to walk the path of your unseen desire. Fiery fire that can burn you to the ground when you don't embrace the nature of your flames.

You have to face the shadow before it can reveal to you the door in the valley of glorious finale.

Sacrifice

Are you willing to sacrifice your fear in order for the true horizon to appear? Are you ready to ask for the forgiveness of each tear, for infusing them with all your fear? For the sake of the ocean, for giving it your drops in fearful devotion...

The blanket that kept you safe and the glasses that determined your view through the anxiety that never was you.

Your cries as the prayers of your soul, to drop all misty veils and rediscover yourself. To create your own sun that's rising and falling, but never yawning.

From now on, always be awake because what caused you to be tired was only the illusion that you hired. The illusion of fear that pulled you back. To go into depth, to ground and nurture your comeback.

hide

The Lion

There is no lion chasing you. That what you associate with the lion is a part of you. It's the strength and power that you will embody when you finally face the future self that has been calling you all along.

Walk into those situations and rooms where your lion is waiting as your strength. The strength that you fear you won't be able to carry. But imagine that you do. Bathe in it and let that emotion bathe in you. By feeling and allowing it to be, you are dissolving the fear that kept you from it. Allow all your emotions to connect with their origin through your heart. Allow all emotions to return home. Feel the wholeness growing inside. No longer empty nor full through the chaos but whole in between everything and nothing.

Note to Self

No more second versions. No more practicing your creative expression. No more measuring to create a certain safety, to prove. This is no science. This is knowledge beyond matter flowing through you. Eternal facts of multiple truths. All shades and colors. Infinite combinations, put together as an individual puzzle without a predetermined image or outcome. You are the filter and creator, building your own world. Your own sense of understanding the infinity of existence.

The wholeness of all would be too much. Let your personal wholeness speak through you and find inspiration and amazement in the magnificent & individual wholeness of nature and others. You cannot practice authentic expression. It's the true perfection and beauty that speaks to you through that first & real-time scribble. The moment of creation beyond the tiny mind but through spirit. All moments after that, all moments that you practice for, are moments without trust in your innermost being. Moments of fear to fail. Moments of control and true imperfection.

Whether it is in art or in love and the connections you have with others, let go. Be mindless. Follow and flow with the first current when it surprises you. The adventure of life can't be planned. It can only be felt.

Guardian Angel

To be vulnerable means to break open the layer of fear that protected you up until here. It does not mean that your heart will break. It never was fragile. The fragility is an attribute of the shell of fear itself. When you make fear the skin and center of your being, you feel its fragility. That's why you run and hide. You are afraid to break, but you have to. You have to break through the mask in which you dislocated your identity. Otherwise you won't be able to connect and experience your true self.

Fear was never you. But it showed you that the path and belief that you invested in were not aligned with your truth. That's why it appeared, to lead you back inside. To compress so deep and tight until you would realize its disguise. Fear truly was your guardian angel. And while you were holding on so tight, it tried to show you your own light. Can you love the fear now and set it free, so that you start being the person that you always wanted to be?

Underwater Tornado

Perfection

Who wants to be perfect? Perfect as in never changing and motionless. Dead like frozen beauty. I am perfect in a different sense. My perfection lies in the nothingness that holds every possibility, every shape, form, and feeling. All of which are right, none of which are wrong. I am perfect in the fluidity of change and the unexpected. I encounter perfection in my exploration of the world. In the nature of personal process and progress. My perfection surprises me daily as waves of unplanned emotions and circumstances. It surprises me as impatience, unrest, addiction, laziness, and worry. But it also embodies me being proud, joyful, dreamy, and disciplined. My perfection lies in my gratitude and the acceptance of all the feelings, forms, and movements that shape my personal days and nights. I am even perfect while acting through my perfect shadow, not accepting parts of me that truly are perfect in their nature. Perfect as in whole. Perfect as in every part has its right to exist. Otherwise it would not be. And of course, in between all those perfect ways, I do prefer some over the others. My preference is what's guiding me on my personal path towards my goals and dreams. Through the wholeness of my being, while accepting the unexpected and often self-rejected parts of myself. I am all, and I am nothing. I am endless transformation inside the heart of unconditional perfection.

The Quest

Searching for the answer to the question that I am,
or am I the answer where no question should have begun?

The quest in my chest,

unrest
full

of desire to know and admire
what seems so far away.
The one truth that shapes every single day.

And what about others?
Can I find myself in them?
In all the children, fathers, and mothers,
to acknowledge who I am?

Do trees hide away my shadows?

Fire, wind, ocean, and land
connect the dots that I don't quite understand.

I feel a sense of belonging,
desiring its prolonging.

I never want to leave this world behind
that brings so many questions to my mind,
but the question and reason for that, what evokes the most fear,
is what's beyond the now and here?

I create hopes and beliefs through the stories of others.
The ones that free me from the fear and let me breathe
through their reflected balance.

Where I once felt the deepness of the dark, I now fly towards the spark.

I can see what used to make me blind.
The darkness is not what I leave behind
but the one that lets me grow.
I am in love with it, in my mind, body, and soul.

In my heart, the below plays its part.

What happened to me?
It seems as if I feel the wisdom of the tree,
growing deep, high, and wide.
I expand and unite.

Into my Eyes

I look into my own eyes through the mirror that gives everything back to me. It holds onto nothing, which makes the mirror the nothingness through which I see myself. I can see everything that I am through nothing that the I is and through nothing that the AM is not. I and eye—nothing as a foggy curtain. Connecting me with everything that it is not and that I AM. Everything that it is in its singularity and everything that it is able to feel through its parts.
And in the blackness of my pupils, I feel the intensity of being. My being that awaits me back behind the form. My being that is always there. My being, that is me, beyond my personality. I can only see it in the darkness of my eye. And I feel its familiarity in the darkness of the night, where I feel most protected, safe, private, and at home. Unseen. But if it weren't for the light, I would not know how that would seem...what existing would even mean.

When I gaze into my own eyes, my body vanishes, flickers, turns light and dark, on and off. Just like the world when I stare at the moon. My morphing body, showing me all that I know that I was and all that I will be. It's radical, drastic, and direct. Without any more layers softening the realization and isness of truth and existence. It lies right there in the eyes. Always observing and looking at itself through other pieces.

When you face your isness through your own piece of mirror, through your own mirrored eyes, you get hit instantly. Its sharp confrontation is disillusioning, bringing you back to the reality of your origin. But it seems so unreal. It's so much and so little that you don't know what to do with it. How to relate to it. And how can you truly relate to yourself?

After you've looked into your own eyes, you will see yourself in the eyes of others too. Looking from all sides always. You and everyone as the self-absorbing universe. Obsessed with learning, knowing, understanding. To be this or that.

Can you be it all?
Can you accept it all?
Can you see it all?
Can you feel it all?

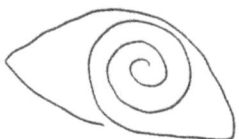

Addiction

Empty remembrance.
The void.
The forgotten self.

Denying the infinite potential
—your instrument.
Unfulfilling a deaf sense
while listening to your drowning sound.

But there is no way away.
You chose the dark door to your core.
To reconnect in discomfort.
The dark spot that is so uncomfortably bright,
holding your light.

A loop of doom.

Unconditional self-love they say.
To love and accept
the behavior that you choose every day
but regret.

Will it dissolve now?
Am I at peace now?
Is it gone?
That part of me that I don't hope to see
with the next dawn.

Is that love though?
No, because you still don't love that particular door to your inner core.
It allows you to see and free the blindness that you are walking with.
And as much as you want to run, it will only make you run deeper into it.
There is no escape.

Avoidance is your dance with the void.

Our facade is that which cries,
the inner victim as the wall inside
between the dark and light.
Just face the other side of the coin
and let go of the agonized devil
that hides in your pleasure-seeking travels.

The dark in us is our mother nurturing us.
It's not wrong; it's right.
And it also believes in the light.

The dark is not your fight;
you chose it as your guide.

Embrace the uncomfortable shedding of skin
and the AM that for so long you have been.

The dying of the old
is your birth back into the I
that sees and knows.
The heart that holds within its name
the art and earth of rebirth.

The empty space remembered
and every part of the body remembers as well.
As it slowly returns to its flowing state, it is letting go of yesterday's fate.

Sometimes you return
in order to burn all that is left.
To drop down once more
and jump even higher
back into your core

—your nakedness.

Shadows

In shadow all forms merge. All color vanishes. There is no more separation. Shadows melt into each other in an instant. Touch each other and become one. The world of shadows shows us that all is and can be one. In the world of shadows, we are all shadows. We are fluid without form so that we can be every form.

Dancing with the bright, a morphing silhouette of body—the dark density of light. Absorbing ourselves. The shadow shows me my wholeness and makes me aware of my blind spot. But from where do I look?

The shadow is my friend. A companion, always by my side. Not possible to hide. Only gone by night. Expanded. Extended into the air and earth. Everywhere and nowhere to observe.

And who am I now? Everything? Nothing? Can I still be in duality? Where will I go, and how do I know what's above and below?

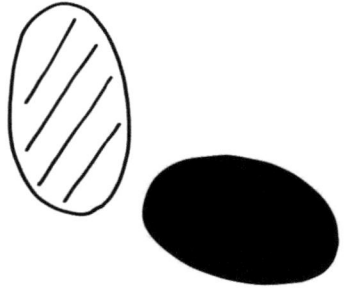

Who are You right Now?

We are fluid,
and we flow
through each
and through others.

We behave,
and we scatter,
being the pattern.

We drown,
we thrive,
we shift,
we survive,
in the constant of change.

We chose the choices
told to us through inner voices.

We are the form—
less
solid
norm.

Nothing at all,
never at fall
but always
in all ways.

Who are you right now?

You are the Story

Evolution is the dying and shedding of the different selves.
The selves inside of you that want to stay who they are.
The seed wants to be the seed, and the flower wants to be the flower.
They don't want to feel the pain of growth, change, and transformation,
but everyone has to play their part in you—the space of their unfolding.

Who are you in this, and who do you want to be?
Through what version do you choose to experience life now,
and through what version do you want to experience life now?
Each is showing you a different perspective.

This is not a race but a place of endless possibilities and infinite landscapes.

Are you the king or queen?
Are you the artist and explorer, a nomad?
Are you the magician?
Are you the farmer?
Are you the villain?
Are you the lover?

Can you be the child, the father, and the mother?

You can be all of them, and you have to be them all at some point.
The flower needs to be the seed first and then many versions more,
before she can fully express her beautiful core.

Can you live in your story and be your own storyteller?
Can you play each character and honor them for their attributes?
Can you keep the balance, and can you be you in all of them?

But who makes the choices?

Black Hole

Am I the black hole? The darkness, not able to see myself and not able to be seen by others? The only thing visible for each of you is my horizon. An illusionary skin of fuzziness, created through the spiraling pull of gravity. My voiceless scream. A fata morgana. Letting you perform a fearful dance around the silence of no escape. Around the depth that I am longing to fill. Not knowing that it will suffocate my breath when I hold on for too long. I send out waves to commune. To consume everyone and everything. To fuel and fulfill my inevitable annihilation through all that I cannot see inside myself. Born from death, I absorb it all while becoming the death for others. To create a new singular seed of infinite potential that births again through its own destruction. Recalibrating the pattern. And the closer you get, the more frozen your pain will become after you went through the burning fires of my outer chaos. Reflecting about life through the decelerated speed of time while you look into the black obsidian of my eye. Ready to burst with each new addition of your particles.

I hold on so tight to everything that I am not. Longing to be, but I have to set you free. Because you were already me. And the pull that we felt was the location that I wanted to share with you as a different point of view. To look together through one eye into all directions of our infinite body and the night sky. I don't have to be it all in order to see it all. Even if it means that we will disagree, I let you be. And we become shining stars again.

Deep within your heart & core lies your own black hole. Your own singularity. Covered by all the reflections as the horizon of skin. Until you collapse and can collapse no further. Death of a star after consuming everything that made you into who you think you are. Now you breathe out, let go, and pulse forth after you've inhaled for so long. The freedom after the fall. To float in between the all. Until you start to breathe in again, to reappear through fear.

Moments

The
moments
that
you
lose
purpose

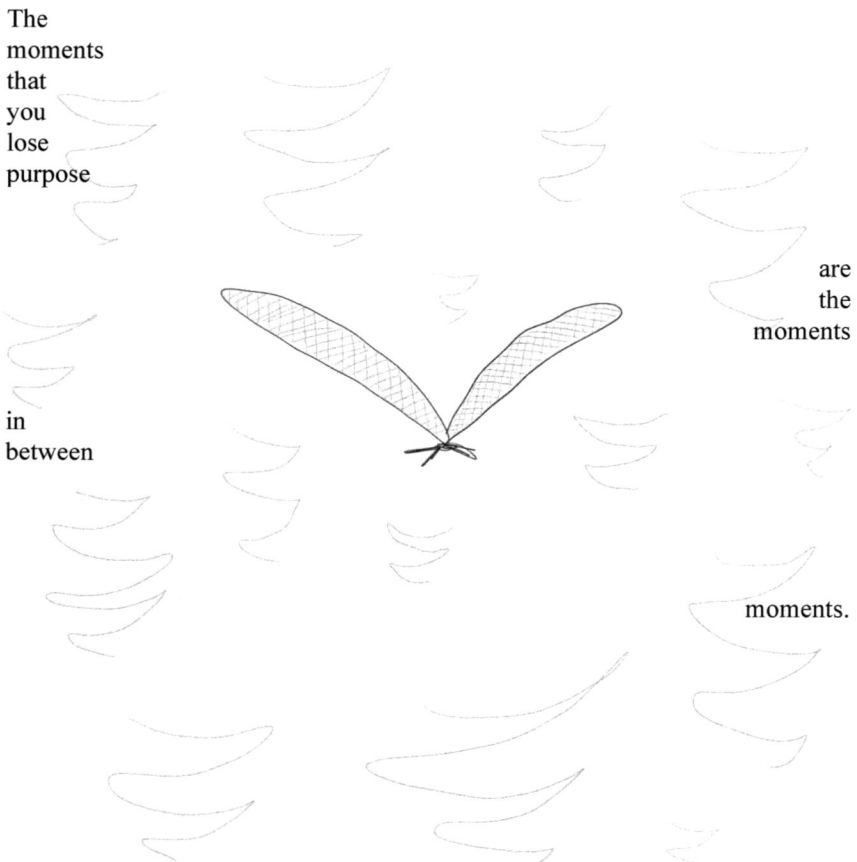

are
the
moments

in
between

moments.

Surrender

I find it difficult to let go of the low,
not always able to allow bliss in what is.

I let my body pave the way
and embrace its growing decay.

I am not afraid to die.
But I wonder why
and how to live with joy the way that I exist
in this vessel.

How to surrender to the way I look
when I do my utmost best to feel good?
Maybe I shouldn't if I could.
Maybe I am just that, and there is nothing
that I must force myself to forget.

To regret that I don't look like her or she,
while they probably have to pay an inner fee
and decay to a much higher degree.

The old wise woman told me that I operate from my light body.
That my body is here, holding a grand sphere,
to ground the new into the old
and spread the wisdom of inner gold.
Because my body serves Mother Earth.

I am able to handle the tense unlike others,
but therefore it is more difficult to dance with the dense.

I am honored, I guess,
but at the same time it makes me feel so depressed
whenever I tell myself that I ate too much or did not move enough.

Instead it's just the energy transmuting through me,
coming from above and below.
Sometimes feeling stuck and sometimes in flow.

It makes me feel so heavy,
unable to escape,
because this is my very fate,
my date with destiny.

Why can't I just be normal and not feel the intensity of this informality?
So much, always, at all times, and even more,
through my very own subjective and self-defective perspective.

Collapse

Bring your gaze out to the horizon.
See everything and let yourself be fully seen.

Sunrises, sunsets,
days and nights.

Free your vision,
soften to yourself,
and collapse into your heart.

Perceive the beauty and love,
the essence in everything.

Be in awe of the variety of forms and feelings.

Observe the ocean.
Set your inner tone.
Integrate.

Let go of the old.
Welcome the new.

A door opens and a new world appears.

What is Love?

Is love the freedom and liberation of things, but also the potential and connection of and between them? Is love the magnetic or the polarizing force? The one that may bring only together what resonates and resounds the same in two or many, through wounds and core values?

Bringing two of the same together to heal. To create something new. Something larger. To expand together as one and to unite in essence? In the very essence that everybody is longing for through others. Longing for self. To unite and connect the parts.

The driving force of all that exists as the only thing that has ever existed.

Human Love

You & Me

I love you;
I am you.

I love you;
I see you.

I love you;
I create you.

You love me;
you create me.

We see each other,
we create each other,
we are each other.

To connect and reflect.

To recognize
oneself,
values,
source,
wounds,
being,
in another.

To heal and come home.

Howl's Castle

Relationships, to share a sense of being and feeling at home.
A ship for a part of the journey to relate, until you sail in different directions.

But there is also a ship like Howl's moving castle. A harbor and point of returning home while on the go. Being your own paths and doors. You both explore the moving horizon from all sides. You are the breath of the castle, returning to yourself. In and Out. To replenish the fuel of the flame that you both share. The flame that can only breathe in through its other part. The reflected heart. The flame that keeps the horizon alive, allowing both of you to thrive. Before all that, you were merely a twig. Not knowing of your potential to ignite, but you could feel the sense of burning already deep inside. Yearning to unite.

Longing

Longing to not be alone on my own but unable to connect with the crowd. It's not because of doubt. There is just no hold, no branch, no one to hold your hand. No one to pull you out of the fast river that spirals inside of you. The river that pulls you deeper into solitude, into your wealth and the refreshing darkness of the self. You can breathe out into the crowd, but you cannot breathe them in. Is my air only the despair of their connection and affection?

I am longing for more than just a dead body, just a flesh body. Longing for more than just sharing my body like a whore. My soul wants to be touched, wants to revive, wants to thrive in love. I want my heart to hold hands while sitting alone on my personal throne. To live my life and build my own queendom while feeling seen by someone else's freedom. Someone that also wants to hold hands. And our hands want to touch the water, the soil, and the sky, being wild and free like birds.

Flying in and out but finding back to each other through each cloud. We share our twigs and treasures as one, not to collide but to combine the wisdom of the divine. Each new twig helps us to sit together in the crown of the tree. From up here we stay grounded and don't always have to fly in order to see. We can see far and wide how everything connects and unites. Just not with us. Because we are supposed to stay on top to guide everyone to water their seeds and harvest their crop. We rebuild Mother Earth's kingdom, where everyone will be able to build their own throne. Based on wild, loving freedom, being together alone.

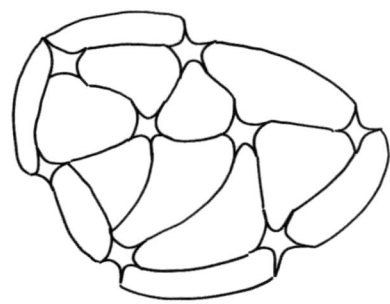

Sinking Logs

All those sinking relationships, built to drown. The reason that you hold on to a sinking ship is that you don't trust your own ability to swim. Why did you choose to get on board? A sense of safety from the ocean of emotion, to stay on top? It's an illusion to only feel the light parts of love. They get less and less because the heavy water fills the boat through the holes of your souls. And isn't this ship even lonelier than the personal freedom that you are trying to escape from? You think that you can choose which way to go, but the true guidance lies in the currents underneath the superficial, spreading into all directions.

Jump.
    Dive.

Get away from that surface level and let go of the other when you don't experience the most incredible love that you dreamed of. You are no water bug. You can't stay on top forever. You are supposed to sink into the depth of your being. If you resist, you will drown. If you jump, you can learn to swim in the currents until you create your own. The treasure of your dream lies at the very bottom of your inner ocean. Well hidden inside your hidden well. The spring of your fortune. Move through all your emotions until you know how to carry yourself. Don't be afraid. The fear is only the surface tension of your waters. Once you jump into the dark, once you embark, you will realize that there is no lurking shark. Only the shadow of water, creating illusions when looking from the top, but once you dive through, it will tickle away that previous shock.

And when you get familiar with the way of water, you can swim with others whenever you want. You are no longer alone in your ocean. Your currents meet, and you become the wisdomkeepers of this eternal potion. It becomes your freedom. Not owned but shared energy that flows to inspire each other. Your courage to face yourself is the bioluminescence that floats to the top, showing people the wonders underneath their sinking log.

Undefine

It's already shifting. Not always accepted but desired by so many. Confused and caught up in the shoulds and coulds but afraid of it being wrong. Not finding oneself to belong without a sense of attachment. Do we really have to choose between the freedom of aloneness and an encapsulated connection? It's not that black and white, because we live with a wide variety of people, wishes, and desires. How to find one's own requirements for love and connection in this scattered world? A world full of old beliefs and traditions that are not even our own. Those groups of people have long been gone. Why do we still live according to their rules and cherish their bloody jewels? Let's melt the old and create a new sacred code. One that activates the patterns of connected freedom.

Move through the lands and seas until your conditioned mindsets cease. To make up your own mind, or are you afraid of what you might find? In communion with nature, you can rediscover yourself, while you never would have thought to be one of those elves. Stories told but not deemed to be true, just so that you can dream a little but stay on the road laid out for you. And you blindly follow through. Is that really you?

It's Okay

I did not fall in love with your mask,
invisible like dark matter
for those who adapt their vision to stay blind,
no.

You taught yourself for so long how to protect that inner part
that is afraid to embark,
made yourself look so strong,
and I felt insignificant, insecure,
and intimidated, like never before.

Until I could hear the broken strings that played your song.

You taught yourself how to hide away from your own self-critique
by using your gift as a technique.
To feel more important
was your way of telling yourself to love yourself,
but you couldn't.

You needed no proof to not allow other teachings of the divine
if there wasn't a clear sign.

I did not fall in love with your mask,
and it could not keep me away either.
I was so afraid, pulled apart
between my mind and my heart,
between self-abandonment and self-worth.

But your soul called mine,
so I told myself that there was no other option.
I needed to know
in order for the direction of my future to show.

This is no critique.
This is my way to not take your way personally.

Because I have to take care of myself
and not fall prey to someone's battled mind.
This is my way to say
it's okay.

I did not fall in love with your mask,
because I have already been
in love with your soul.

The Sun and the Moon

We protect our wounds and heal them in the shadow and harsh light of others. Together we are like the sun and moon, while our grounding center is the earth. Days and nights spinning around each other's axis. A dance of hide and seek to heal and breathe through the hurt.

Homecoming

I came from Earth, and I deserve to feel her all,
every raindrop and every single snowflake that's about to fall.
Every breath of wind, every sound in the desert,
each wave of the ocean and all possible emotion.

She has two poles and so do I,
as well as a core,
a hidden well,
and a sky.

Each part is its own world, and together they are one.
Every body, every cell—a magnet.
Needing each other, feeding each other.
Repelling what doesn't serve their dwelling.
What serves and resounds the same
rules this never-ending game.

Balance out and dissolve each cloud
that covers the paths between body and mind.
The path of the child,
and that 'kind' is your heart.
It's the love that connects your parents and poles,
making you whole as the soul
while creating through their presents.

But if I am whole on my own,
if I am one through my heart,
can my soul still be a part?
Could it be that, at large, I am the true north to someone that is my south?
A similar soul, living in a different house?

Such an intense attraction and reflection
that there is no denial of the connection?

A part of me that I did not know,
as something that I left behind in order to refind?

Beyond body, beyond mind,
only my heart knows this kind.
The mind tries to understand and defend,
but no logic shows what you sense and feel.

This path is supposed to heal you, to be true.
To balance and dive into the wholeness of your soul
so that you can grow and expand together.

To unite and give up the internal fight that kept you small.
And even though it seems so much,
you already have touched yourself in the mirror.
It feels like home.

Let go of the confusion; this is no illusion!
Your mind just cannot understand something of this extent.

It's rare, beautiful, and true. All about you.
You, learning to shine, to help others
and to experience the divine.

The fear only shows you the walls inside
behind which your truth might hide.
Walls that the child built up to protect,
ready to be broken down and reflect.

No longer reject what you desire;
light up your internal fire
of who you are, who you want to be,
and what you want to see to feel free.

The black forest of the night is now lit up to unite
the mountaintop with the roots of the tree
and the desert with the ocean.
Make it happen with devotion.
Be the fire and spread your sparks
to ignite all the other hearts.

Am I too much?
Am I too little?

Can I meet myself in the middle?

Is there a middle
between day and night,
between light and dark?
Can we meet each other in the heart?

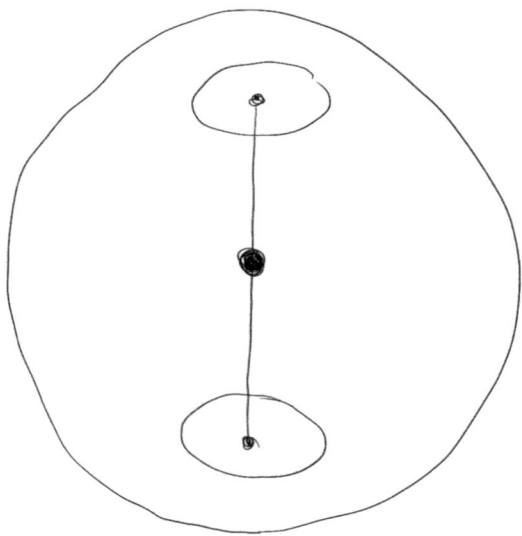

Let It Be

Let them admire you while you are loving yourself.
Let them admire you until they find their own balance within.
Let them admire you until they are no longer afraid to start a new beginning.
Let them admire you until they can love you.
Because your glow will make them crazy.

And for you, this is a time to go deeper within yourself too.
This is no waiting.
This is being.

Forgiving

The only person that you ever have to forgive is yourself. Forgive yourself for creating the arousal inside through the expectations you´ve had of others and the meanings that you´ve placed upon their behavior. Forgive yourself for your own behavior. Forgive yourself for not seeing that all those actions represented the reflections that you needed to see in order to know who you truly want to be. But don't forgive yourself for feeling all of this, because feelings are the road towards your inner bliss. There is no other way out of the chaos than by being in it.

Forgiving yourself is for the giving to yourself, in love.

I've got the Love

I've got the motherly love.
I've got the fatherly love.
I've got the brotherly love.
I've got the friendship love.

I've got the hateful love.
I've got the painful love.
I've got the necessary love.
I've got the silly love.
I've got the healing love.

I've got the self-love.

and now,
I feel you.

Let's change the World

When I first saw you, I wasn't aware,

and when you told me
that you could feel everything,
it was the first time that I felt seen.

Someone that was just there.

I could have tried to hide,
but I already felt at home in your presence.
Not for the sake that you saw me,
but that's another story.

You probably do not realize what you did for me
in those beautiful conversations
with all the unpleasant confrontations.

You taught me about authenticity,
even though I could see
that not all of your fears
were yet to agree
with your own truth.

So that's why I am here.
To show you what I learned from you,
to embrace myself in grace
as something that now you have to face.

It's your turn to collect what you have earned
through all your troubles, fears, and pain.
We found each other because we are quite the same.

Holding past and future for the other to see
while guiding us back into the now to be.

And when we have accomplished that mission for ourselves,
we can lead the rest of the world into this inner wealth.

You told me that's what you desire most,
to change the world and free everyone from their sorrows.
But the only way for this to work,
to reach all wounded hearts,
would be your own.
Because that's where your infinite potential starts.

Part III

The Void

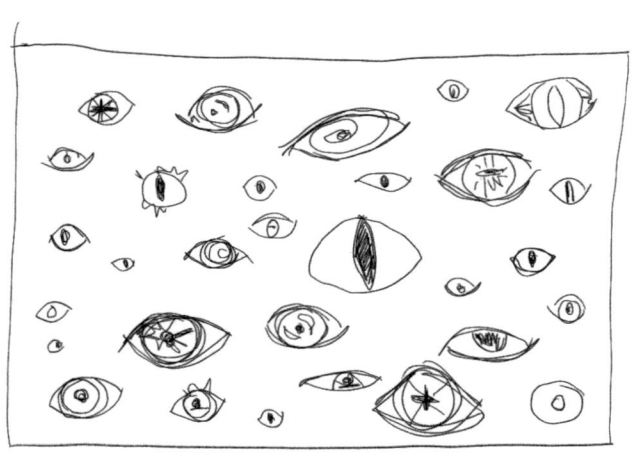

The Eye of the Storm

*Each Storm cleanses Itself from its own Chaos,
to free the Inner Eye and expand the Silent View of Clarity.*

The Body of Things

The formless mind holds the growing shadows of the heart that is shining so bright, creating everything through the light. The body of things as the dark light, the magnetic love of atoms. Electrical discharges of attraction and nonconnection. The dream of touch. New states of being to be born through the joining of shadows in form.

The sense of the I. The question of the self. The personal awareness searching for its own place to belong, while the collective I is shifting in between the norm, as breath and water flow through each form.

The One

There was never a first version of anything.
There is only one version of everything.
All exists always in the now.

And there is no existent state of nonexistence, no opposite of source.
There are only endless possibilities and transformations within this realm,
all realms,
and through the illusion of time.

It's the unity and connection of all.
Existence that creates through love as love.
Love creating itself.

And we flow through it, as it,
from the center
back to the center,
in each emotion.

The one that changes,
the one that scatters,
the one that creates the illusion of separation in order to experience itself.
The one that creates within and through its own creation,
through the ocean, through humans, and all beings.

Breaking into as many pieces as possible in order to reflect as much as possible.
To see itself in its reflections from many sides and all sides.

In judgment with itself,
in hate, joy, sadness, greed, loneliness, and hope,
through all thoughts and situations.

Expanding while longing for its own heart through the other,
until it recognizes itself again completely
in its essence,
as love.

The Eye of the Storm

Through attraction and repulsion, connection and affection, the two drops long to become one in the silent eye of their shared storm. They are the forces that connect low to high and the ocean with the sky. Once we become that center in the middle, the zero point that enables the sound of the fiddle, we will be free. Because all emotion connects and dissolves back in and through the birthing ocean at its core.

Unrealized love — the black heart — the space.

The void and the pulsing spark.

No matter if it is day or night, dark or light,
by becoming the totality within,
you no longer live by the tide;
you no longer need to know how to swim.

A Dream is a Dream is a Dream

Once you embody the emptiness,
you no longer sleep.
You are awake in the dream of day.
You can see the illusion at play.
The lucidity of darkness.

And there is no more fear,
because you know that all of this is not really here.
But you are, round after round
making your own creation sound.

And when you go to sleep, you travel beyond time.
All the everywhere is here, and it's all mine.
I speak to you.
You speak to me.
I observe all the different versions,
all bodies and creatures
as infinite teachers.

I no longer exist then,
I only exist now,
and I remember it all like a spiraling flow.
In this I am the eye of the storm,
connected to experience every moment and version
in sensual form.

Inside my center I am still;
the only thing that exists here is nothing
but divine will.

I am the dreamer and the dream, always now.

Silent Lake

From Carbon to Crystal. Dark Ashes until the Phoenix is Reborn.

You Are

What and who would you be,
if no one would have ever given you a name?

What and who would you be,
if you would have never been born into a family?

What and who would you be,
if no one had ever taken care of you, for you to feel free?

What and who would you be,
if you wouldn't live in a house, decorating those walls?

What and who would you be,
if you couldn't see the reflection of me?

What and who would you be,
if you had forgotten all your history?

The System of Love

In the moment of realizing that you are all of it, you feel lonely, spacious, and senseless. The life that you lived up until this point appears meaningless all of a sudden. And everything that you planned to do does so as well. It seems as if its only meaning is to understand the experience of the heart. To experience the system through the pulse. Becoming aware of oneself through the vibrating parts. And the realization that this version can't be all that is.

From now on there are moments and days that you feel nothing at all. You let everything and all emotions flow through you by becoming the portal that makes you feel empty through each fullness. The only things that truly make you feel alive are the fundamental laws that create the veil that keeps the totality away. Even though you silently long for it—the totality of love, to be all and nothing. Fear serves as an intrinsic part to keep you in the closed loop of your heart. The running and pleasure-seeking, trying to distract yourself from the unachievable love. As long as you don't allow yourself to be you and as long as you deny the fear to be here.

You are floating so far ahead, observing in disconnect, so deep in the heartspace—the void. Senseless beyond the senses. You wanted so deeply to understand it all. Life and this reality. The game of ... you. Would it have been better to stay blind? Because now you belong to the lonely kind. No longer wanted to follow and crawl but to know yourself, and now you know that you know nothing at all. While the other hidden games appear to stay hidden, you can feel their presence. Because pieces of those come through you to you since you opened your heart as the dark portal that connects each part in your higher soul.

It's at this moment—now—that you have to give new meaning. Become the creator consciously and return to your game with a new set of rules as new uplifting fuels. To connect all the characters, worlds, and games. All the valleys and beings of your dreams, visions, and intuitions. Parallel versions of you, parallel versions of me, and landscapes out of this reality. To uncode and decode the program with the codes that you receive. Your heart knows the way, and you know it too, since your greatest passion is shown through it to you.

Once the mind has settled in and transmuted the sense of newness that it has always been in, you will find that the emptiness is refreshing and its aliveness is not as intense. Rather gentle. It's you as the space that feels itself everywhere when you expand from your physical anchor into the world. Becoming one with all, so free. You are the never-ending story.

Beauty

How can I write about something so delightful,
silently prideful?

Full of light,
even in the darkness you never hide.

Empty and full
of breath.

Subtle,
delicate,
invisible but there.

Inside,
outside,
everywhen,
everywhere.

Not able to touch,
not able to see,
not able to grasp you
in your entirety.

But I can feel every time,
in every being
and every piece of art,
when I am drawn towards you
with my heart.

There is no wanting, needing, nor attention seeking.
No scream.
No cry.

Beauty,
you seem so innocent and shy.

You can be found in every aspect and every expression,
always leaving an impression.
You are the essence of sadness, anger, grief, joy,
and many more
because you are bound to each core,
and each core is bound to you.

Most bright when being real, authentic, and true.
You are me, and I am you.

Just an Idea

What I am is just an idea.
All led by love and held back by fear.
An idea that my parents had one day.

I don't have to explain myself to you, because I can't.
All of life is way too much to comprehend.
But I want to let you know what I think and feel,
as the only experience I deem to be real.

Maybe we can attach our knowledge of the insane.

I want to find out why we have a particular name,
why we end up here and not there,
and why we have so much food that we are not willing to share.

I want to know how to alter life and how to deprive negative beliefs
from one's promised life.

I want to know why I want to be seen,
but only in my ripe season,
for all the right reasons.

I want to know why I long to be understood in my innerstanding of the world.
And why I want to be as outstanding as I can.

I want to know if Benjamin Button can be real
—why growth doesn't go from old to young.
Or does it?

It's all about growth,
to be seen and touched as the sweetest version,
to bring about new seeds from the old life
in order for young generations to thrive.
To fairly share and create a global balance
where no one is in despair.

In the end, life is much more simple to understand.
So simple that we don't even have to comprehend.

Just look at the trees and bees,
at the rivers, rain and clouds.
Feel the breeze while gazing at the sea.
Feel the warm and cold
and internalize the symbols of the old.

Why do we carry the idea that we are not part of this world?
Only believing to be led by his name,
God—our own mankind mind game.

We search too far away in our head,
while all that's in front we already forget.

We are born through nature—ourself,
and we keep believing that we are something else.

There ever only was one single thought.
Inside all is the same.
One mind.
One love.
One flame.

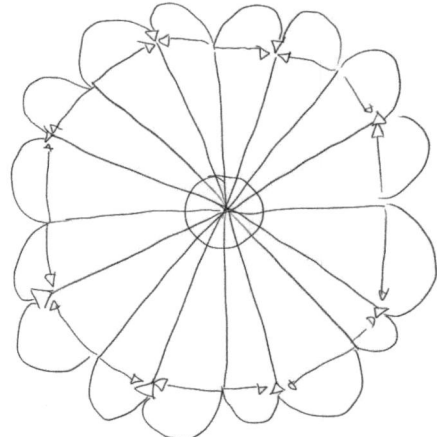

Who Am I?

All of a sudden I realize that I am here in this moment where I've always been. Where I feel like I just woke up from a dream, already forgotten. And the reality that I woke up to is one that I can't remember either.

Where do I belong? All that I see doesn't look like me, and how do I look? There are only the reflections of my own refractions that cast back to me a distorted image. Even more distorted through my definitions. Is that where my truth lies? I rather disassociate with the outside world that's supposed to serve as the mirror for my identity. All that moves past me and all that does touch me. Where to hold on so that I don't get swept away?

I feel so blind, sensing the layers, hearing the prayers. Who am I? I want to move out of my blind spot, past the mountain that can only be alchemized by me. I surrender. And for the first time I can see my fate. But silent is only the first view before my hue starts to create ripples, showing me my path. And my reflection is once again of the past. I will never see myself as I am, because every moment it's a different version all over again. Am I in the illusion of change, or is it time that is within me? All while I remain eternal as no singular part. United as all in the body of the divine heart.

THE PROTAGONIST

PROTECTION

Empty Love

The feeling of nothing.
Still and motionless.
The silent fate to create
through the dark mirrored lake.

Conditions and labeled connections,
focused only on surface-level reflections.

Blocked emotions that don't know how to flow,
because we hold on to everything that we think we know.

Rather feeling something unreal than nothing at all.
The fear of losing the sense of emotion
that controls us as a bewitched potion.

Can you feel the space that created you and that you are within?
Can you let the outside flow through
without it having an effect on you?

Full of empty love
means handling life without gloves,
to truly feel the fullness of touch.

Once you make that shift,
you are no longer able to be in love like in the past.
Not with anyone.

Because now you can feel the larger system that you are.
The high and the low as your highway to know.

But when there is one of you, there should be another,
since this play exists of father and mother.
Poles connected through their souls.

Masters as equal partners who know themselves through their hearts,
connected to the emptiness that is playing in each part.

The Spider and the Web

Like a spider, pulling the web out of its own body while crossing its created paths again and again. Navigating itself through the expanded self as the structure that creates all the story's. Through layers upon layers and all crossroads of density.

In this web, some points are easier to escape than others. But is there really an escape from the self? The spider knows where to linger and where to catch itself in triumph for another plot twist. Consuming the lives that nurture the infinity of creation. Freshly produced threads that inside and out continue the blueprint. The web is where the creator pulls you back into the center of your origin. The seat of observation, where those that have died are born again.

Carefully structured into sections as the spiraling wheel. Desperate for its expanded creation—the outside world, in order to hold itself together. In order to relate and give reason to faith. The clock of infinity that does not plan but allows the flow that carries with it the momentum ever evolving.

You are the expansion within your own creation. Getting to know yourself always in all ways, as your own temple within the template. You are the shimmer of the web that only shines in a certain hue when the sun lays its rays upon you. When you start to fly in the freedom of your ray, you realize that you are more than just red, blue, or gray. You are the white after you've absorbed the light through the dark. Now you can start to ignite the spark, and your hue will become a unique rainbow.

You want to be caught and held. You don't want to escape the essence of the spider's web—love. But when you are in search of it, you might illusively place yourself into avoidance after all. Because this love is different. This love is not what you expect. This love is essence, lifting up the veil and confronting you with your mask, its traits, and the person that you think you are. It surprises and catches you in your fall of lost hope. Caught by that web, again, once in a lifetime. It has to, because it needs you to remember so that you continue to build new layers of heart-led expansion. It was you who set this all up, and the love that you now feel is out of your own cup.

You are the web, the spider, and the thread.
You are the love, the lover, and the loved.

The River

Do I move through the world, or is the world moving through me?

I change. I shift. Nothing else. All else is me. The shift suggests the movement. Time, a property of infinity. An opportunity to create all that is already created. An opportunity to think about yesterday and hope for tomorrow. An opportunity to live a life while dreaming with open eyes. I wake up on repeat. Within myself. Within my own permanence. Now and now and now. I don't expand; I shift. From one image to the next. From one dream to another. Now. Any idea as the next possibility. I am the fear(s), I am the person(s), I am the soul(s), I am the angel(s), and I am the angle(s). I am space, I am time, I am word(s), and I am world(s). I am what it means to be a me. If I want to return, I drown myself and take another turn. I overflow and dry. As a beginning for new ends, I die. I am the river that gives life to all, showering under its own waterfall.

Unconditional Love

The Essence of Romance lies in its surprising Factor.

Enough

It's impossible as a being to choose with whom or what you fall in love. It seems to be the greatest mystery of all that we cannot figure out. But love is much more than just a regular emotion. It's not an equivalent of anything or any feeling, but it's the sum of all as their origin. It's the core frequency of existence itself, and it's unconditional. Unconditionally supportive and unconditionally accepting of whatever belief and experience you choose. While the fact that you do exist is proof of your worthiness of all that you desire. View yourself as enough. Just enough is already enough. Start right here and right now, because that's the only reality you will ever have. Everything else in the past or future is a connection to parallel and possible events that you call into the now, non-physically and energetically, while moaning for their loss or longing for their materialization. A state of not being or having enough when you don't feel gratitude while dreaming about it. A memory embedded in your subconscious that gives you the opportunity to contemplate who you want to be and how you want to live.

Unconditional Self-Love

Unconditional self-love is the freedom you give yourself to be all that you are and all that you want to be, which is all that you are supposed to be. Your soul's and your heart's desire. Every possibility exists there. You create your own reality, play and experience from it, in it, as it, and through it. Freedom as a feeling that true love can never take away because it is the same. In a paradoxical way, it allows you to create the necessary limitations to build your dream and to change into your preferred version while you accept what comes before.

Heart Space for Others

To accept and love the other as they are without any expectations. To see their essence beyond their limiting beliefs, behaviors and feelings. To see them as the love that they are, no matter how much they are able to express it at the moment. This love and heart space that you hold for them doesn't require any action, attention, or pleasing from your side. It's a space in which you allow them to be free in whatever way. Free from a force to change. You are just there, as a spacious presence.

You give the other the gift to be seen without judgment. Seen for their soul and potential in the now. For all that they are, all that they could be, and all that they choose to be. To feel appreciated and accepted for their existence itself.
In this space of yours, the other might first have to learn how to feel at home when they have never experienced the safety of true love. Like a blinding light that makes every one of their shadows visible, even if they don't want to look at them. Underneath their surface, they can feel through you what they truly have to do.

This love of yours can be experienced as a void of uncertainty, though. Nowhere to hold on to, no condition to adjust to, no reason to run from. The isness of your heart is overwhelming and reason enough for the other to run while you remain you. Until they choose to transform their silent hopes into loud beliefs and loud fears into silent trust.

It's nothing that can ever be possessed or lost. It's a love that holds the realization of who you are at your core, in contrast with how you used to perceive yourself. It's a state of being that requires no effort. Once you allow yourself to be every version that you used to be, that you are, and that you want to be, once you allow your past to have taken place as it has, once you allow all the challenges and the self-images that you hold against yourself, that's when you enter the heart space, and that's when you become the love for yourself and others. All while maintaining your invisible boundaries through authentic expression and self-validation. You don't require anything from anyone anymore in order to feel loved. And through that you are able to accept everyone in their own place.

122

Wholeness

Love in its pure form knows no borders.
It's infinite like the universe.
It expands to experience every aspect
in all directions and dimensions
until it remembers itself.

But for that it does not return;
it does not contract.

It reaches another level.
A new membrane and layer
from which it continues to grow,
to store more information, knowledge, and creation.

Growing.
Remembering.
Knowing.
Forgetting.
Expanding.

From one cell to a community of cells
—a new horizon of body.

We are the cells that forgot, and we are the cells that start to remember,
in matter and mind, through the heart.

The Garden

New Love. Love is not easy. It means every feeling. There is no one story to it, and no knowing how it is supposed to go. With each person and constellation of individuals, it is experienced differently. No constants but everflowing versions of one another, with one another. To learn what they both want and don't want. To be.

And sometimes, most times, always, relationships play a part in revealing and healing your wounds. Each person acts as a fertilizer on your path, through the landscape of inner weeds. Until you pull out what grows too deep and high.

At some point you might not even need the other anymore to show you your weeds. Someday you don't have to be a gardener anymore, but you become the garden yourself. Connected to everything inside, sensing all the needs so that your wholeness can thrive. You will start to accept the parts that you used to reject. Now serving as the very nurturers of your being. Rooted deep, they reach your heart like no other part. They make you feel so vulnerable, where in reality that vulnerability is your strongest card.

Then, when you are thriving so well, your landscape might no longer be big enough. It wants to expand and connect once again with other land. With another person that also became their own garden. And there is a silent river flowing through the two. A connection that can't be denied and that nurtures both of you. If you want to grow together, you neither have to lose yourself nor leave your garden behind, but you will find a new sense of wholeness. To accept one's weeds, to get to know each plant, each fruit, and each thorn. All beautiful and important on their own. Together you create an oasis only known and felt by the two, and a secret pathway to it that guides both of you.

I Love You as in...

I love you as in: I can take a step back, zoom out, and try to see the entirety of our connection. To see in what layers and parts we do connect. If in wounds or in transparent and honest interests. I notice the intensity of this analogy. I feel the push and pull, but I will not move with those forces out of desperation anymore. To float above has taken quite some time, and sometimes I drown in it again. At least I try to not lose myself in the electricity between us. I flow with it when I choose to and when I feel that you no longer hold your current back. Let us flow freely because that's the nature of things. We cannot drown in love nor fear when we translate everything into verbal communication between our individual states of observation. We can witness every degree of this unspoken bond and take a conscious look at the parts within ourselves that are illuminated. We can choose if we want to continue to operate a certain way or if we want to change for the path ahead, as parts of us have been activated to awaken by the other. A continuous mix of running and longing, of fear and love, until we own up to ourselves and our hearts.

Both opposites helped to show me who I truly want to be and where to place myself. To find my true center within, not only living on, as or behind my protective skin. To fully accept and love myself again. At least more than enough, despite all of my past sins which were never meant to hurt anyone nor me. It was a set of beliefs that did not allow me to see my inner throne and my heart as the most important part. The origin and guide of this existential ride.

I love you as in: I don't require a response from your side. I just love you in every way you choose to be because you're allowed to be free, just like me. And yes, a part of me does desire an interaction. But I don't let my desires rule over me. I can feel them and still be at peace with the now and what is. The only moment that will ever exist. And in this moment I am fulfilled with love. Love for myself, for you, and for life. All the love that I feel for anyone or anything, what I see in you or them, is the love that I am.

Your reflection shows me my past and my future, in which I am the center of it all now, reflecting and projecting. By seeing where you are, I can see where I have been. And thanks to you, I can see through this new door that has opened within. The door to my core that allows me to love even more. I no longer long through my wound. I am perfect and complete, so there is no reason to compete. And I have to search no more because what I was looking for was me on higher grounds. The outside only showed me those reflections of my wounds. I don't deny that I loved through them, because the wounded connections helped me to heal and grow. It wasn't easy, though. Because every birth deeply hurts.

And now I am here. Born and evolved through that fear. Eternally grateful. No longer hateful towards other versions of me. I have set myself free. And the only reflection that I will now attract is the most honest and true love that I won't ever reject. Because I am true and honest with myself now. I am worthy of it, and that's a vow.

I love you as in: Our love is free and can be whatever we want it to be.

Part IV

Second Birth

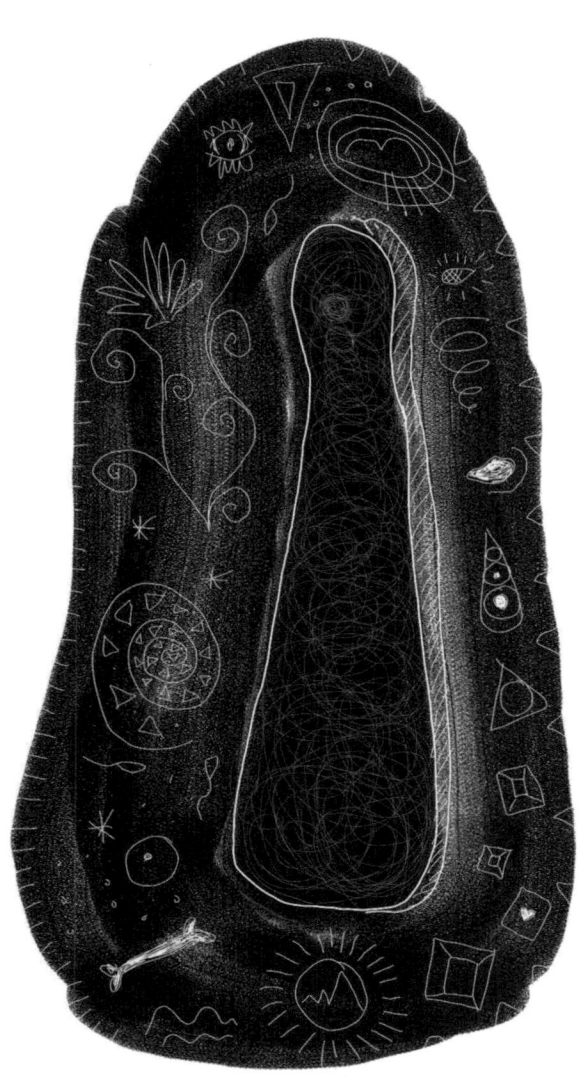

Emerging from the Womb once again,
but this Time it's my Own

*Feel your Form, see your Energy,
and feel the One that sees the One that Feels.*

The Womb

The first womb experienced a new mental horizon,
stepping onto the land and connecting with the air
through plants being aware.

The womb was never just the ocean;
she was supposed to transcend.

To go from dark to light,
from low to high.

And we are still with her right now.
Nurtured through existence itself.
Through earth and spirit.
Through all connections, inspirations, and ideas.

We are the planet transcending,
giving life to new versions in every moment.

And we hold all the layers that came before us,
mineral, water, plant, animal,
each one carrying its own wisdom.
While learning from each other,
we predominantly learn through them
until we feel the wholeness of our being
as earth again.

We are the womb that becomes aware of herself in all her facets.
She is us, and we are her,
experiencing ourselves multidimensionally.

I Dream

When I sleep, I am awake, and when I am awake, I am asleep.

I dream,

inside,
outside,
night and day,
each time a different theme.

I dream
that I can fly,
sometimes
up high
above Earth.

And I see all of you crying for help.
You want to climb higher,
but the trees are your limit.

Look at all the old shapes,
all the old forms.
Look at all the wisdom that transforms.
Look at your body and look at Mother Earth;
your sky is down there.

Where?
There where the horizon hides
behind your inner mountain.

I dream;
inside each stone
I feel at home;
through each crystal
I see;
as comparted elements
I be;

through Mother Earth
I birth.

I dream,
and the ocean whispers.

I remember how I felt
when I was the salt,
when I was the tree,
when I will be the bird.

I dreamed, and I heard
the sound and voice of my heart,
beating so hard.
A pulse that moves through every part.

It moves through my dream.
It has always been
and always will be
my day and my night.
In my heart they unite.

Delusion

Is this real or a delusion? All that I see, all that I write, and all that I feel? I want to speak my truth, but aren't there so many contradictions in this book already? It's because all my versions want to have a voice and speak about their particular choice. But if they do, who am I, and when do I know that it's me that speaks to you? This book is a collaboration where I just am, them and them and them. Even if they battle and fight, no part is wrong, and all of them are right. In the end it's about what I choose as the truth that shall lead me, and mine is the one where I believe in romance.

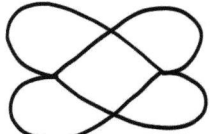

I own my Alone

I desire connection, but something that I do not desire, instead utterly require, is my solitude. My sense of self. I love the person that I became, the person that I am! I love my life and my friends. I love the sun and the rain. I love the joy and the pain. And very much I love my home as the personal space that I can call my own. I love all of it. I love the art that I create and the realizations that are my faith. And yet, I still feel alone. Whether surrounded by people or while being at home. The reason why I choose to be on my own is because people don't know how to relate to me. I feel like my orbit lies far outside the crowd. Enjoying the silence in the darkness, far away from the loud. Am I a faraway star? So far away from their realm of mind, not being understood. I am yearning for my own kind that I may never find. So that's why I am rather alone. Not to shy away, but to allow myself to carry my crown. I will invite you in, but only if I can completely relate to your deepest well hidden underneath all sin. Layers of fear that hide your magnificent dragon skin. I truly believe that you and I are here to push away all this fear that covers up the beauty of each. Our breath of fire might hurt a little because it's sharp and pure, but it's required to burn away the thick grease that keeps everyone in infinite unease. We are here to free the self-esteem that allows each one to embark on their dream that makes life worth living.

You are Here

Rays of sun shimmer through the outer layer of the womb. Through the surface of water they reach you unfathomable, as you rise up from the deep, dark ocean of the old into the new world of wonders. A horizon no longer untouchable. The mystery that you embody now makes you able to see through the veils and currents. To realize more, to become aware of the shore, and to let go of the fear. But you are still allowed the swimming in order to show all others this new beginning. You are here to float in between, back and forth, for the expansion of Gaia and the connection of worlds. Dreaming awake to infinitely create.

We would have Drowned

If we had stayed,
we would have drowned.

The ocean learned how to breathe
the pulse of life.

It learned to fly,

and humans became the horizon
between body and mind,
earth and sky.

We are the third angle of the triangle,
where water and air as the

–

un

–

a

–

void

–

able

–

as the
force of life,

flow through its creation.

Where the first womb meets the second
and where dark and light come together as the rainbow of scattered light.

My Higher Self

When I am up there
in this other conscious flair,
I can feel more.
I know when things will happen more or less.
Moments that I feel, before they become real.

I can hear the silent voice
that never screams through the noise
but whispers in clarity.
It tells me what to do
and leads me in each step.

It also calls your name,
which was the first thing I truly felt that made me aware
of this higher affair.
Happening in my own air,
my own breath.
My spirit.
It's a place out of time,
where every déjà vu lives within the cosmic mind.

It's the shared world of me that most times
I wasn't supposed to see,
but it wants me to remember.
To know what is and what will be,
without having to use my fantasy.

I don't have to search any longer for my truth
through empty imagination.
My script was written long ago,
and I am heart-led by my higher soul.

It speaks to me because it's time.
I am ripe enough to work for the divine.

New Ways of Breathing

*Holding Ourselves back from what we want to express
makes us the Ones that deny Themselves.*

Success

It may appear so far out of reach. You may believe that you are not born for this. That your family's future heritage is not one of rich lightness. But it's written all over the place, all over the world. The rich people did not become rich in their wig. I am talking about the ones that hold themselves authentic and with bliss. Those that inspire. The ones that we admire. They are your messengers. All of them followed their hearts through all the heavy mud. Because their heart knew that joy won't keep them stuck. And joy doesn't mean that you have to wait for the money because it pays off already right now, in love. Don't you forget, you can't be any richer than that. When you love, every other wealth will fall into place. Keep believing in your dream and do what lifts up your self-esteem. You already have it inside. Now you create it in form to relive the inner ride.

What would Love Do?

When you stand at a personal crossroads, no longer knowing which direction to take and what decision to make, ask yourself,
What would love do?

When you find yourself in a situation that feels like you are losing yourself,
ask yourself,
What would love do?

When you don't know if you should run, fight, or hide,
ask yourself,
What would love do?

When you step into another's wounded field, not yet healed, and they scream, and they cry, don't immediately reply. Instead ask yourself,
What would love do?

What would love do when it could act through you?

For the Sake of You

Share the love that you are and love all that you are.

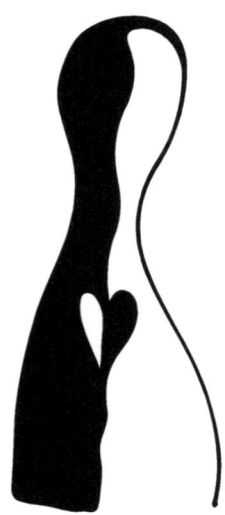

Confidence

From insecurity to security, from confidence to self-doubt, from order to chaos. I thought letting go was my goal, but it's about being confident in my doubts, my fears, and my chaos. Being confident in being the constant of change. Being confident in my worthiness through all the feelings that were gifted to me. Being confident in all my inner equals and all their messages.

Integration

Discipline no longer works. It's going with the flow now. No forcing where the force doesn't want to go, but letting the force flow. To allow whatever it wants you to do. Walking this new path will be fun when you let your heart take the steps.

You are not lazy when you surrender. When you feel that your mindless push of mind can't go against the current. You are now being filled with endless fuel. With sacred fuel that only fuels your truth.

When it's resisting, it's not where you're supposed to go. Embrace the change of what your mind couldn't think of. It will be much more rewarding than you think. Old ways crumble. The doing, the living, the pleasing. But you can still see it all around you. All those pleasure traps. It's the ultimate choice that you have to make, and you already know that there is only one way to go.

Your legs might hurt at first because you are no longer walking in circles. When you take off your shoes and let the feelings settle in, you become one with the path through your sensitive skin. And while you rest, all the new steps will appear underneath your feet.

The Crystal

You are the crystal within your soul. The crystalline part that refracts its light to create an experience through its own mental prism. As the holographic reality surrounding you. The heart as the connection to your pure essence, unique frequency, and individual soul flame.

Through the connection of the heart, you can express this truth of your flame into the world once you put the pieces back together. Therefore, view the totality of your thoughts, experiences, and emotions through unconditional self-love. You will be offered a kaleidoscopic view of those pieces that create your personal mandala. A mandala that holds all spread seeds with the opportunity to grow and expand from yourself towards yourself. From forgetting through the unknown darkness back into remembrance.

You are your own diamond with your heart as the umbilical cord between you, your higher womb, and the realization of this infinite safe space of soulfulness. It also connects you with all the other hearts and souls that together form the web and multidimensional crystal of reality and creation.

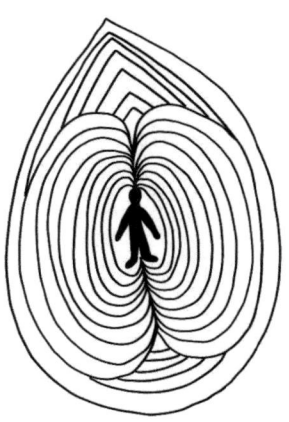

Careless

Like ebb and flow,
care moves through the wounded and healed
parts of my soul.

Arriving at my heart.
Days of unwanted obsession,
forced oppression.
And days of total disregard.

I just want my inner peace.
Focusing on me, solely.

I no longer care what you think and do,
even if my heart cares for you.
I no longer look. I let it all be.
I set myself free.
Regardless of your soul's presence,
that's always with me.

I don't make myself something that I am not.
I no longer try to impress,
just in case I might be seen.
I won't make this my leading theme.

A second ago I was so afraid,
and now there is no more care
for how anyone might mark me.
I just share all of this crazy me,
because I have built my own ark
that navigates me through the dark.

You can drown in all of me,
or you may join me at sea.
I don't care, but if you do,
I might as well welcome you.

The Spell

I am not here to put you under a spell.
I am here to show you how to break yours.

The Last Step

I have to try,
even if the closer I get,
I am more anxious than ever
that my dream will pass by.

I have to put it out there now.
That, what is most vulnerable to show.
This very book and all the texts
in which I declare my love to you.
I just have to, because I do.

Risking all that,
what I haven't acquired yet.
But if I don't, I won't feel alive.

There is no other price than going forward.
And there is no end.
It's only the journey defending itself
as if there is nothing else.

I preach so much about fear,
but it's also present with me here.
I feel it deep in my core
like never before.
It lets me cry,
makes me crazy;
I am so afraid to try.
But I hope that my hopes will praise me
as I let the old me die.

I can't give up on you.
Not you, but the love that I feel,
made known to me through you.
A reflection. You are my lake.

I can't give up on myself now,
because this life is too precious.

I want to feel it all the way I mean it all.
To feel all that I said and all that I didn't.

I let my heart fly to show y'all
that it can swim in the air
and float far above despair.

And if I fail,
I might put my love in jail.
For the first time.
Forever. For me.
So that it can try again to break free.
But that's not something that I hope will be.

Existential Love

Invisible like Air, if it wasn't for that Golden Shine.

Knowing

You can never know someone or something completely through thinking, because there is no unconditional knowing possible in the singular mind. Only by sharing knowledge and wisdom through the network of the many can a larger knowing exist within the collective consciousness. It's a wholeness through the multitude of singulars. Knowing is about communicating and exchanging between the different points of view that form this whole. We might not like certain perspectives, but existence is infinite, and as such it does not stop at your own viewpoint. It's not about being right or wrong, but it's important that you follow what feels true to you in order to play your part in the larger body. Connect with those that feel like home and with whom you form a particular organ together. Accept others, knowing that they form a necessary part as well in order for the larger structure to stay in balance. Any fight between two is just a fight against you. Of course there are systems that do not operate in an interest for wholesome growth. They invade other parts without realizing that they destroy their own hearts. Stay in your truth through love. Because only then will you transform harmoniously.

Deep connections arrive in your heart before you have ever really conversed by mind. Your mind cannot love. Your mind can never fully process this magnetism. The only knowing as love lies in the heart, and the only thing that the mind can do is to translate it into words. But it will always remain a filtered translation.

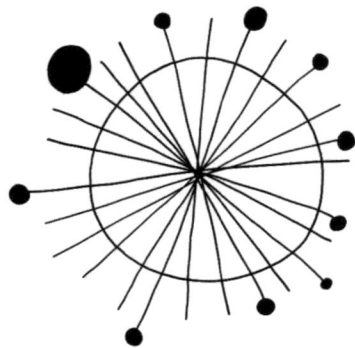

Life - The Game of Love

How to play? You already do. You can choose, however, if you want to keep playing it through your character or as the whole you. Take an inner and outer distance and observe your interactions with people, places, and events. But predominantly the interactions that you have with yourself. How to break out of such an infinite game? Out of the magnetic loop that carries you away with its current through each emotion, while always longing for love. And even when we seem to have figured it out through all the turbulence, we still want to return. We still want to take that risk to feel—the beauty of pain and the intensity of it all. The journey that liberates the self from its own creation. Over and over again.

But there is a secret gateway. A path that allows you to keep playing without ever having to lose, win, or cheat. A love that is no longer conditioned by the player. You become the portal—the heart that doesn't take any sides. You allow everything to flow through you freely. Loving it all as the space that you are. No holding on to nor being the current. But allowing the current to be. You are the space where the current is free. Where each fight can resolve inside. During days and nights you receive dreams and visions that guide you in your ambitions. You think that you shift in and out of characters and worlds, but it's the reverse. It's them that flow through you since you freed yourself from the curse.

And this is exactly what everyone is longing for. The freedom of the heart space that allows you to face it all without taking a fall. Love that is free of any form, taking on its own shape, away from the conditioned norm. It comes to you through all your connections and different levels of reflections. Now you grow even deeper into the art of the heart, as souls together even when physically apart.

Needless to Say

Needless to say,
I don't need you,
but I love you,
and the world needs us.

The Melting of Souls

Any friend can ground you back into the character that you play in the relation-ships with others. Nonetheless, it all feels distant now because of the new reality that has opened up inside. Through all the moments that you spent in your co-coon. Like looking through one-sided glass: so clear, the disconnection.

Once you reach that edge of insanity that reveals all your depth to you, there is no other version left. You fall and keep falling through the now nonexisting layers of space and time. You keep falling into you, all happening in your own momentum through the space that you create. Through your own unfolding, re-expanding into eternal singularity. The only one character that is left is your awareness, becoming more and more acquainted with itself through its own mist. Sometimes as light as a heavy cloud, rainy and dewy, sometimes thin as air, like a breath that flows everywhere.

And for that first and last template of your being, there is only one reflection left. The one and only fit for your truest version. One that goes with you into the very essence of depth. You can feel them even before both of you went through the last layers of snow. But it has already started, the melting of souls. It's that per-son, that was ever only meant for you. You, as the formless naked body, absent to be touched, only able to be felt and recognized by the one that (dis)embodies the most similar hue. And you recognized them. Beyond time and space, that particular scent, only your heart could sense. As it was a sacred, stored memory asleep inside, by your side, each and every day and night.

A forgotten conviction made true for you, by you, as you started to remember yourself and listened to your essence as the silent voice. Conveying the only choice: to embody your soul, which brings about answers to all the others as a whole.

Delta

In my mind I feel like a lunatic for the fact of not having you here, wanting you here. In my heart it feels like grief for the person that is dearest to my soul. I can feel it all, but I cannot see the places where we are and have been in this far field inside, the world we call forever, ever since we forgot. I feel dry tears each day that you are not by my side. But you are, otherwise I couldn't feel you from so far, right here.

I never imagined a love going so deep. And all of it even without having touched, kissed, or freed the words from the heart that longs to expose itself. To show you the river of magnetic blood that propels me towards you. But the timing to fully connect hasn't been right just yet. While our minds are in the momentum of bridging the wisdom of all tears, we are led through our shared delta.

Heartfelt

Your heart will first see it as it feels it, before it can believe it.
Because the heart works the other way around.

You make my World Sublime

The second I looked into your eyes
I knew your soul, I knew your shine,
and I knew our hearts had already kissed
before your lips will touch mine.

How could I forget what I knew?
I can't imagine carrying on in life without you.

It's not your body; it's your soul,
and I know that something tries to connect us as a whole.
As two in one through the song of hearts
that doesn't want us to be separate parts.

After the purge of the past, minds and souls merge.
I have the desire and urge to feel your body,
to kiss you, and to hold your hand.
I want to hug you free from your fears.
I want to give you my heart
and listen to every single one of your tears.

I see me in you and you in me.
I can't spend the day without longing for us to be free.
Free in infinite love, free in space.

I never want to have to imagine your beautiful face
because I rather gaze into your eyes.

I love you, and I always did.
The first moment that I saw you, I started to remember it.

Let's explore each other's landscape together,
naked—in body, heart, and soul,
your skin on mine.

Why do you make my world so sublime?

I don't want us to be apart.
Let's be two parts together,
through every storm and in any weather.

I never felt something as strong as with you.
I wish this to be true.

Thank you for sharing the expanded view
in which I can discover more of myself through you.

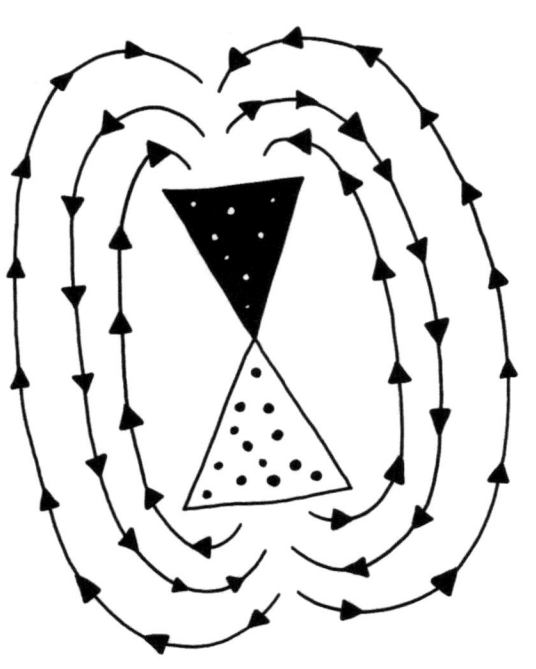

Epilogue

A Message from Me to You

It might look like I carry a lot of self-confidence when I share all those words of wisdom. And I did become so much more confident indeed, because I started to love myself. But keeping up that confidence is not always as easy as it looks. It requires daily reminders of my own worth, especially when I feel overwhelmed and at my lowest. I had to learn to become comfortable with the highs and lows, with the vulnerability and the resistance of the small self that's afraid to be seen or touched. I no longer want to hide from others nor myself, even if I feel like it. I am pushed to release the pressure of the continuously incoming flow of information that's expanding not only my sense of self but my idea of life and all that is. We came to walk on this path together, and those texts happen as much for me as they do for you. It's the wisdom of the universal heart flowing through my vessel, urged to be shared.

Don't be afraid, because fear is no longer part of that new version of you. Fear is the self-designed illusion, a veil, that helps you in your journey of rediscovery. The dark cannot diminish your light, but it offers you a stage where you can step into your truth and start to shine. It takes so much time to get used to the insanity of it all until you notice that you no longer have a sense of time, especially in those moments where you feel like you are losing yourself in between the definitions about your being. Continue to trust in your heart's calling and allow the transformations to happen. After all, they are your birthright. And you know that it's time now; otherwise, you wouldn't be reading this book. It's time to open that heart of yours again to unleash the second beat of your destiny.

Epilogue

My dear Poetry

My dear poetry,

I write to you, through you,
while you are flowing through me.

You give me the needed sense
to process what it means to be.

You give order to the infinite chaos that I need to define,
to assign meaning
to the meaningless nature of my living primetime.

My dear poetry,

you are a structured blueprint for me.

The infinite in written word,
unspoken,
until I give you my voice.
Endless options,
so much choice.

You give shape to the yet-to-be-informed.
You are the sound of silence,
about to be performed.

You are the word that sounds in any leaf and any bird.
You make the grass green and allow neglected parts to be seen.

My dear poetry,

your tongue of art brings beautiful images to my heart.